The Point of No Return

**Tackling Your
Next New Assignment
With Courage & Common Sense**

Other Books by Rick Renner

Spiritual Weapons to Defeat the Enemy
Dream Thieves
Dressed To Kill
Merchandising the Anointing
Living in the Combat Zone
Seducing Spirits and Doctrines of Demons

The Point of No Return

Tackling Your
Next New Assignment
With Courage & Common Sense

Rick Renner

Pillar Books & Publishing Co.

P. O. Box 471692
Tulsa, OK 74147-1692
1-800-542-BOOK

The Point of No Return
Tackling Your Next New Assignment
With Courage & Common Sense
ISBN 1-880089-20-3
Copyright © 1993 by
Rick Renner
P. O. Box 472228
Tulsa, OK 74147-2228

Published by
Pillar Books & Publishing Company
P. O. Box 471692
Tulsa, OK 74147-1692
United States of America
1-800-542-BOOK

Cover by sigma graphic design

Edited by Elizabeth Sherman

Printed in the United States of America.

Dedication

To Dr. Bill Bennett, for all the wonderful things he taught me and imparted into my life as I served alongside of him. Thank you for teaching me, instructing me, correcting me, and giving me a godly example to follow in the course of my life and ministry. Most of all, thank you for teaching me to always give the glory to Jesus.

Table Of Contents

Table of Contents

Preface

The term the point of no return is a navigational term which could be illustrated by the following example. When Charles Lindbergh flew across the Atlantic Ocean for the first time, he reached the point of no return when he had burned so much fuel that it was impossible for him to turn back to America. At that point, he only had enough fuel to continue on toward Europe, and it was impossible for him to return home.

The point of no return will always contain the elements of risk, striking out into unknown territory, and many times accomplishing what looks impossible. For obvious reasons, not many people experience it.

As Christians, when we have expended many years of prayer, faith, and hard work, believing for a dream God has put in our hearts to come to pass, and that dream lands on our doorstep one day, we reach the point of no return. There is too much invested and too great a knowledge of God and His plan for our lives to turn back or disobey. We must go forward, because to turn back would mean the destruction of our lives and the nullification of our purpose.

As I write the final page of this new book, there is no doubt in my mind that we are right in the middle of a tremendous miracle of God. We have passed the point of no return again and again to get here, and we are passing the point of no return to do what we are doing now.

Here in my office, I am gazing at a huge map of the former USSR, looking at all the big red circles our staff has drawn on it. These red circles indicate all the regions where we are now broadcasting the Word of God on television to the former Soviet Republics. Although we were told this was impossible, we have found that when you know the will of God and do it, anything is possible with God!

I am so glad we didn't listen to the negative voices who said all of this was impossible and that we shouldn't attempt it! Had we heeded them, we would have missed all the wonderful things God wanted to do in and through our lives.

As I grow in my own Christian experience and walk with the Lord, I find myself taking a more practical approach to finding the will of God and doing it. We are doing what others would call crazy, impossible, and even insane, but it is working!

We are discovering that doing the "impossible" isn't impossible at all if you understand what steps to take, how to proceed, and, just as importantly, how fast you should move ahead. If you have the answers to these questions, and if you have a strong spiritual foundation for your life, you can do anything God asks you to do, regardless of how hard or difficult it looks to the natural eye.

If your heart is saying, "I'm ready to do whatever God wants me to do with my life," then *The Point of No Return* is a book that will speak directly to your heart. Students, businessmen, ministers, teenagers, parents, husbands, and wives will benefit from reading it.

Anyone who is challenged to be more excellent and effective will be helped by this common sense approach to taking on your next new assignment from God. This book is for people who are ready to end the status quo in their lives and do something significant. It is for people who know God is calling them to go higher, faster, and further, to pass beyond the point from which there is no turning back.

It is my prayer that after you are finished reading this new book, you will never be happy to stay the way you are right now. I pray you will rise up in faith, accept God's next impossible task for your life, and boldly move forward into previously unknown territory. Only then will you discover the favor, blessing, and miraculous power of God!

If I have just described you, welcome to a life of faith and adventure! Every aspect of your life is just about to change. You are about to encounter your own personal "point of no return"!

Rick Renner
Jelgava, Latvia, 1993

Now after the death of Moses the servant of the Lord it came to pass, that the Lord spake unto Joshua the son of Nun, Moses' minister, saying,

Moses my servant is dead: now therefore arise, go over this Jordan, thou, and all this people, unto the land which I do give to them, even to the children of Israel.

Every place that the sole of your foot shall tread upon, that have I given unto you, as I said unto Moses.

From the wilderness and this Lebanon even unto the great river, the river Euphrates, all the land of the Hittites, and unto the great sea toward the going down of the sun, shall be your coast.

There shall not any man be able to stand before thee all the days of thy life: as I was with Moses, so I will be with thee: I will not fail thee, nor forsake thee.

Be strong and of a good courage: for unto this people shalt thou divide for an inheritance the land, which I sware unto their fathers to give them.

Only be thou strong and very courageous, that thou mayest observe to do according to all the law, which Moses my servant commanded thee: turn not from it to the right hand or to the left, that thou mayest prosper whithersoever thou goest.

This book of the law shall not depart out of thy mouth; but thou shalt meditate therein day and night, that thou mayest observe to do according to all that is written therein: for then thou shalt make thy way prosperous, and then thou shalt have good success.

Have not I commanded thee? Be strong and of a good courage; be not afraid, neither be thou dismayed: for the Lord thy God is with thee whithersoever thou goest.

Joshua 1:1-9

Chapter One
The Point of No Return

Have you ever earnestly longed and prayed so fervently for something, every cell and fiber of your being waited in anticipation for that thing to happen, and then, suddenly — *it happened!* — and things began moving so fast that you felt like your head was swimming?

Stepping out in faith to accomplish something new and adventuresome, something you have never done before, can be scary. It's not scary because it won't work or because God won't be true to you, but simply scary because it is something you've never done before. It's the prospect of entering into unknown territory that makes you feel a little shaky on the inside.

Have you ever felt those conflicting emotions, like an earthquake in the pit of your stomach, as you approached the moment when you knew you could not turn back — that moment when you knew the past was gone and you could only press ahead to do the will of God? After all the years of praying for this moment to come, it's finally here! Reality is striking hard and fast, and you wish you could turn the clock back and think about it for just a few more days, but that is no longer an option.

Your time to step out in faith has finally come.

The days when you were able to pass the buck, when you could back up, slow down, turn to someone else to lead, or just say, "I'll do it later," are gone. Yesterday's luxury of saying, "Someday . . ." is a memory from the past. The day of delaying the inevitable is gone.

You have just reached the point of no return!

There are many times in our lives when we face the point of no return. Some of these occasions may be small and seemingly insignificant, such as taking your first dive off the diving board or making your first entrance in a school play. Others may be greater in scope, like resigning from a secure position with a large corporation to start your own business, or having your first baby.

Whether large or small, I have found that each time I have faced the point of no return, that same overwhelming feeling of simultaneous excitement, anxiety, and eternal destiny has welled up from the center of my being. This complex feeling arises because we are stepping beyond what is familiar and comfortable into the unknown, in the same way that Peter stepped out onto the raging sea to walk toward Jesus (Matthew 14:25-29).

I honestly believe that, had I not chosen to take those smaller steps into the unknown in my earlier years, taking the incredible leaps of faith the Holy Spirit has led me to take in the most recent years of full-time ministry would have been very, very difficult, if not impossible. The Bible says we should not take lightly our small beginnings, and this is one servant of the Lord who has the greatest respect for their small beginnings.

All of the early choices to trust God over my own thinking or preferences built my faith to the point where I could begin trusting Him in situations that would not only affect me, but others around me. I have learned that when God calls you beyond the point of no return, it is because He has a plan waiting for you that far exceeds your wildest imagination.

My Own Experience With
The Point of No Return

Many years ago, Denise and I were pastoring a very small church in Arkansas, when God spoke to me that it was time for us to move on to the next phase of His plan for our lives. I remember how I felt when I told Denise we were resigning from our church, without any knowledge of where we were supposed to go or what we were supposed to do! Some of our family members, and at times even Denise and myself, thought we had lost our minds for undertaking such a leap of faith.

Our church was small, and we might have been living below the poverty level, but we did have a house (a very old one) and friends who lived around us. Stepping out in faith to resign from that church was a monumental undertaking for us, but we knew God was changing the course of our lives to move us forward in His perfect plan.

As I stood in front of our little congregation and told them we were resigning, my stomach churned. I realized that, once our announcement was made, there was no turning back. *This was the point of no return in our lives.*

After our resignation, we spent thirty days praying and waiting on the Lord, until our spirits were able to discern His direction for our lives and ministry. The Holy Spirit took me back to the vision He had originally given me years before. He tenderly spoke to my spirit, "I've called you to teach the Word of God to My people."

When God first called us to a teaching ministry in the United States, I was petrified at the thought of launching out into this new unknown territory. I had a gift to teach the Word of God, but I had never taught outside of our little circle. Therefore, when the Holy Spirit spoke to my heart and told me we were to start teaching the Word of God to believers nationwide, it sounded as big as Goliath must have looked to little David.

To begin with, who knew us? We had been living in a small Arkansas town for five years, and we weren't well-known. Living in that little town didn't exactly put us in the mainstream of activity, and because of this, we weren't known by many people outside of our tiny circle — and I do mean *tiny!*

When I stood in front of our family and told them our next step in life was to start a national teaching ministry, they logically asked, "How in the world are you going to do that when no one knows who you are? How are you going to support yourself as you get started? Do you know how to do this?"

My answer to all of those questions was, "I don't know!" Their questions didn't bother me, however, because they were voicing the same questions I was privately asking myself! All I knew was that the Holy Spirit had spoken to my heart and was preparing us for a new adventure. When He spoke to me and I said, "Yes, Lord," faith was imparted, and I was ready to carry out His plan for my life. I was excited, scared, thrilled, petrified, happy, and shaken to the core all at once!

Stepping out into a whole new realm was exciting and scary! I had so many of the same questions my family and friends had, and more. "What is the first step we should take? How do you begin a nationwide teaching ministry? How do people become familiar with us so they will know to invite us to their churches? What if we take this step of faith and then absolutely no one wants us to minister the Word of God in their church? How am I going to feed my family and pay our bills until our teaching ministry gets established?"

As we first took our steps of faith to obey God, I felt that earthquake in the pit of my stomach! We were doing what God wanted us to do, but because it was new and something we had never done before, we felt that natural, shaky feeling that you experience when you step into brand-new, previously inexperienced territory.

All I knew was that I had a word from God to start this new adventure in our life. We were sure God had spoken to us, and we commenced on our new pilgrimage of faith, which has reaped incredible supernatural fruit ever since. Hundreds of thousands of books and teaching tapes, many video tapes, other teaching materials, and thousands of speaking engagements have occurred in our ministry since we passed that point of no return.

Most significantly, acting on that word from the Lord was preparation for the next major step of faith God would require of us seven years later: *moving to the Soviet Union!*

The Ministry Expands to the USSR

After seven years of traveling all over the world to teach the Word of God and seeing God do miraculous things with our lives, gaining a good reputation in the United States as a teacher and author, and preaching in over 2,100 meetings, we were finally achieving what we thought was "success" in our ministry. The struggles of making ends meet were coming to an end, and we were receiving 900 invitations a year to come and speak in some of the nation's greatest churches.

We bought the house of our dreams, our staff in the Tulsa office was as committed to our ministry as we were, and my books, tapes, and videos were being distributed by the hundreds of thousands. The ministry was fulfilling a need in the Body of Christ, which was very gratifying, and God was blessing us personally beyond our wildest dreams. Everything was perfect in our lives, and we were enjoying every minute of it.

Then God spoke!

While on a mission trip to what was at that time the Soviet Union, the Holy Spirit spoke to my heart and said, "Because of all the people who are being saved in the USSR right now, I am calling you and your family to live here and to teach the Bible to believers who need to be established in the foundational truths of My Word."

I nearly fell over when the Lord said this to me! Astonished, I asked the Lord for *further clarification.* He spoke to my heart that, because of the outpouring of His Spirit upon the USSR, the need for good teachers was imperative immediately!

I understood that, in such a time as this, when possibly the largest door for the gospel in the past one thousand years had swung wide open, the need for balanced and experienced teachers of the Bible, who could put new believers on a solid foundation of truth, was an undeniable necessity.

Still stunned and somewhat aghast, however, I asked, "Lord, have You forgotten what we're doing in the United States? Do You remember that You called us to teach the Word in America? Maybe You overlooked the fact that we have an office staff in Tulsa that needs to be paid every month? Have You forgotten the fact that I don't even like missions?" But my real fear was not leaving America or doing missions. I would do whatever God required of me. My real fear was financial.

I kept thinking, "How am I going to support a ministry in the United States and Russia if I never have any meetings in the United States? Will our partners forget about us and stop contributing to our ministry? Will I be able to pay our bills? How am I going to pay the salaries of our staff in the Tulsa office if I'm living on the other side of the world?" Nevertheless, God's firm voice kept whispering to me, "This is the next step in My plan for your life. If you'll obey Me, I'll make sure you are covered financially."

This was a great test for me. I was comfortable in my present ministry, and I was happy and proud of our new house in Tulsa. I was enjoying a measure of notoriety among people and ministers in the church whom I had admired and respected for years. Now God was asking me to put all of these things aside and follow Him into the unknown again. So . . . I bit my lip and recognized that it was time for another big step of faith.

Denise and I sat on the couch in our family room, and we talked and prayed. We were American to the bone and were proud of it! We were raised in the days when the Soviet Union was our big enemy. We could both remember being taught in grade school how to protect ourselves in case of nuclear fallout! We could recall being rushed down hallways and stairs into the basements of our schools during practice drills to protect ourselves from a military onslaught of communism.

We were sure there was no better nation in the whole world than the United States of America, and naturally, moving to a country that had historically killed Christians didn't sound appealing, especially since we now had three young sons! But sitting there together, we saw how God was truly calling our family to move to the USSR.

As we worked through our fears and recognized this was God's will for our lives, a flood of faith and excitement began to pour into our souls. We were thrilled just to think we would be teaching the Bible in a place where the people had known nothing but atheist communism. Only God could do such a marvelous thing!

Our fears turned to faith as we recognized the hand of God in our lives. The realization that we were going to be a part of a major outpouring of His Spirit in the last days began to sink into our hearts. We were supernaturally filled with courage to begin this new adventure!

I called our families and staff and gave them the news. They were shocked, but the same grace that was upon us came upon them. They took the news like troopers, and asked what they needed to do to help us make this major transition in our lives. I called our own pastor to talk with him about our decision, and he said, "This is God's plan for your life."

Everything was moving ahead peaceably and nicely — and then I knew it was time to make our first public announcement about our big move. I was at a meeting out of town, and standing in front of that crowd to make the announcement was exciting. The leaders of the church came forward and laid hands on me, prophesying how God was going to use us in the Soviet Union. My adrenaline was flowing and my emotions were at an all-time high!

After the meeting, I went back to my hotel room and called Denise to tell her the big announcement had been made. After I hung up the phone and sat in my hotel room — *all alone* — the reality of the announcement I had just made began to hit me like a semi-truck! Every ounce of fear that had been hiding in my soul over the years suddenly decided to pay me a visit, and my thoughts began to race with questions.

"What have you done? Why did you make such a stupid announcement to all those people? What if your partners stop supporting you because they won't see you as often? What if the communists begin to persecute believers again, and your family is caught in the middle of a horrible mess? What if you can't support your family or your headquarters in Tulsa? What if this. . . . What if that. . . . What will you do?"

I kept thinking, "Stupid! If you hadn't publicly announced what God was calling you to do, you could have disobeyed and no one would have known it but you and God! Now, if you don't follow through on your plans, everyone will think you're spiritually unstable and don't really know the voice of God."

I felt absolutely trapped. Suddenly, I understood why the Apostle Paul frequently called himself "the prisoner of the Lord." Like Paul, I was chained to a new commitment to Jesus Christ from which there was no recourse. This new commitment to obey the Lord was final and binding.

I began to feel the same kind of earthquake in the pit of my stomach that we had felt years earlier when we left our church in Arkansas. It was also the same feeling I had had when we began our teaching ministry in the United States. Furthermore, the big earthquake I felt in the pit of my stomach the night I made the big announcement had many after-shocks. I had scores of smaller tremors that shook me for weeks to come!

It wasn't a lack of faith or distrust in God that created those shaky feelings. It was merely an awareness that God was calling us to do something bigger than ourselves, something we had never done before, and something that we surely could not do without His help. I felt completely and utterly dependent upon Him, and fully aware that without His help we would fail.

Because we are creatures of habit, stepping out to do something new is always a challenge. When our little world is shaken by God to expand, it nearly always creates temporary feelings of uneasiness and discomfort. Thank God, those emotions eventually pass as you follow Him. And somehow, I personally believe that one of the main reasons He calls us again and again to the point of no return is to remind us that He is our total source of security, that nothing is impossible with Him, and that we can do all things through Him.

That's Not the End of the Story!

We began to seek the guidance of the Holy Spirit to answer all of our questions. The specific place we were to call "home" in the USSR was Jelgava, Latvia, so we began to work out the best means of communication between Latvia and our U.S. office. We even developed an emergency plan in the event that our family was caught in the middle of a political crisis.

We scrimped, saved, and used our money as wisely as possible in order to make the move without burdening our ministry and partners. We found a buyer for our dream house, put most of our furniture in storage or gave it away, gave our ministry van to a missionary in Mexico, sold our family station wagon, and broke the news to our boys that we had to find another home for our beloved family dog.

After a year of preparation, packing many boxes, and tearful good-byes to family and friends, we finally walked onto the first of several airplanes that would carry us across the globe to our new home in the former Soviet Union. Our hearts rejoiced that we had really done it! We had put aside our doubts and fears and all our creature comforts, and we had obeyed the word of the Lord! A major milestone in our lives had been passed!

When we arrived in Jelgava, we settled into our new home in no time at all. We began teaching the Word of God in a local Bible School and preaching in churches all around our region. Our boys began picking up the language and relishing every hardship. To them, shoveling coal to keep the house warm or boiling water to take a warm bath was the greatest fun they had ever had. God even blessed them with a new dog!

News of Denise's beautiful operatic voice traveled quickly, and she was invited to sing at Stalin's Conservatory of Music in Riga. We stood in awe as, after Denise sang and testified of Jesus, many tearful hardline communists received Him as their Lord and Savior.

Not only were we enjoying ourselves and truly feeling at home, but to our delight and pleasant surprise, we began a marvelous and miraculous love affair with the people there. We had expected adventure and challenge, but the joy of ministering to these precious people, and the deep love we had for them from the moment we stepped onto Latvian soil, was an awesome extra dividend!

Right before our eyes, lives that had been painfully and cruelly oppressed spiritually, mentally, emotionally, and even physically for over seventy years began to be wonderfully and beautifully transformed, healed, and set free by the power of God and His Word.

Knowing how we could have missed all of these tremendous blessings from the Lord, we breathed a sigh of relief that we had obeyed Him and had chosen to take the big leap of faith again, pass the point of no return, and follow Him to the former USSR!

Stretching and Growing by Leaps and Bounds

Amidst all this joy and excitement about our new life in the former USSR, and just as we were beginning to feel at home and comfortable, the Holy Spirit spoke to my heart *again!*

He said, "Now I'm going to tell you why I *really* moved you to the former Soviet Union. The next part of My plan for your life is to begin teaching the Bible on *television* to the peoples of the former USSR!"

My mind was shaken at the very thought! Even in America, I had never had the slightest desire to minister on television. Furthermore, I didn't know if I could legally teach the Bible on television in the USSR. Just two years earlier, I would have ended up in Siberia for such an attempt. I kept thinking, "Come on, Lord! I've already obeyed You by moving here! That was a big step of faith! And now You're asking me to do this, too? At least give me a month or two more to adjust!"

Then, all of a sudden, I knew exactly where I was. I had been there many times before. God was calling us onward and upward and the clock was ticking. We were once again approaching the point of no return. Life was changing again, only this time the change had come sooner than the last. God had allowed seven years to build our teaching ministry across the United States before He called us to move to Latvia, but He had only allowed us a few months in the former USSR before He began to speak to us about a television ministry.

We knew there were no options for us if we were going to obey God with our lives. We also knew this meant our faith had to grow, we had to change, and we could not look back. God's will had been revealed, and we could not pass the buck to someone else. The churning in my stomach started again — but I knew we had gone too far in our walk of obedience to stop now!

Still, a television program sounded crazy to me! I didn't know anyone who had attempted to start a television ministry in the Soviet Union. Because the doors to this former bastion of communism had just opened, and the West had only begun bringing in ideas and technology, there was no one to whom I could turn to ask, "How does the TV system work in the Soviet Union?"

In actual fact, *no one* knew the answer to this question, not even those who lived there. Because the mass media had been KGB-controlled, the manner in which the public communication system worked was a big secret. Thus, we had to learn all of it by ourselves as we did what the Holy Spirit told us to do, traveled to places where He told us to go, and talked with those to whom He led us.

We jumped on airplanes, flew from one end of the Soviet Union to the other, to war zones, and to regions where no American had ever been. We spoke with television Deputies, visited with powerful former communist leaders and television technicians, and began to negotiate contracts for the program in regions the Holy Spirit had put in our hearts.

What we were attempting to do sounded so insane, even our loyal interpreters thought we were a little "over the edge"! Absolutely no one had attempted to do this before. Again, despite all the voices who said, "This is impossible," we proceeded with the Lord's direction and began broadcasting the teaching of the Bible on television.

At this writing, we are reaching more than 150 million people every week, including the most remote and Muslim-dominated regions of the former Soviet Union!

Establishing a television ministry in the former USSR once sounded like an overwhelming challenge, but after doing it for awhile, it has grown to feel quite normal. The fears soon left us, and we began functioning as the Holy Spirit commanded us to function. We have learned that, as long as He says, "Do this," or "Do that," we can do it.

If you had told me we would have done this several years ago, I would have laughed out loud and said, "You've got the wrong guy!" Now we know that the impossible really is possible, and that there is nothing more thrilling and satisfying in life than tackling the impossible — and winning. Through this, we have learned we can do the impossible every day, and it can seem easy and natural!

Your life becomes a supernatural life when you obey God.

He calls you to break camp and move your tent to higher, tougher ground, into a new realm of obedience and faith. Initially, it is challenging and even frightening, but once you've conquered those initial fears and established your obedience in that new realm, you settle into God's ordained place for your life, with a higher and deeper level of peace and trust in Him.

Remarkably, as soon as you are settled into that new place, it's probably time for you to move up higher again! Just like the last time, once you've obeyed the Lord in another new realm and the fear fades and your faith moves up an incredible notch, you are probably ready to receive another new directive that will continue to develop you, challenge you, and conform you into the image of Jesus Christ.

Following the Lord and obeying His instructions never ends in the life of an obedient believer.

Right now, my family and I are doing what God has commanded us to do. For the present time, the earthquake in the pit of my stomach is gone, even though I am doing something that would have scared the life out of me several years ago! Moreover, we are doing it with absolute peace and confidence in our hearts.

But I am sure of this: if we intend to continue obeying the Lord, it won't be too long until the Holy Spirit puts another challenge in our hearts. Then, we'll leave this present comfort zone to enter into the next God-ordained phase for our lives. I can hardly wait! *We'll have to face the point of no return again!*

You Can Do More
Than You're Doing Right Now

It is rare that I would spend so much time in a book talking about my family and myself, but I felt that my personal testimony was valid and necessary for the opening of this particular book.

There are some areas of knowledge and wisdom in the Word of God that must be lived in order for understanding to come. That is why I am using my own experience with "the point of no return" to introduce the subject of this book. I have learned that when it comes to being a doer of the Word, there is no substitute for experience. The following chapters are literally the pouring out of the Word being lived out in my own life.

I have learned we can do whatever God asks us to do. Most often, it is much more than we are doing right now. God's plan is to conform us into the image of Jesus Christ. If we are not using our faith, allowing His compassion to work through us to bless others, or living a life of obedience to His Word, then we are not cooperating with God's plan to change us and transform us into powerful Christians, who live and act like His Son.

Believe me, you can do much more than you are doing right now. The only thing that stands in your way is giving into inexperience and the fear of doing something you have never done before. If you choose your doubts and crippling anxieties over faith and trust in God, you will miss the life of adventure He has planned for you. He may not call you to live in the former Soviet Union or to start a television ministry, but the plan He has for your life, for your family, for your neighborhood, or for your business, is every bit as significant and exciting.

Our spiritual success isn't measured by what we do, but by whether or not we do exactly what God's asked us to do.

I'm sure Noah never dreamed God would use him to preserve the seed of mankind by building a big boat. Abraham was living a comfortable life when God called him to make a journey that would establish a new race of people. I am certain Moses never dreamed he would topple an Egyptian empire and then receive the commandments of God. Do you think Elijah greatly cherished the thought of confronting the prophets of Baal?

Little Mary, the mother of Jesus, was just an unknown girl who received a word from God, obeyed it, and changed history. Her life and all of our lives were radically altered when she knew the Lord was speaking to her and she boldly declared, *"Be it unto me according to thy word"* (Luke 1:38).

The disciples, most of them uneducated simpletons before they were called by Jesus, surely had no idea that the good news they preached would be used by God to shake the very foundations of the Roman Empire and *"turn the world upside down"* (Acts 17:6).

The Apostle Paul, nicely settled into his Judiastic lifestyle, clearly had no idea God would call him, change him, and use him as a champion for the faith he once loathed and raged against. Yet, this one little man was used in such a mighty and powerful way, we are still eating the fruit of his revelations today.

All of these men and women of God did far more than they thought they could do. Our great God is a Master at taking insignificant lives and making them significant. But if any of these believers had chosen to be bound by their human limitations, they never would have accomplished any of these things.

What we must always remember is that when God calls us, He also equips, provides, sustains, and empowers us to do more than we think or even imagine we can do.

Have you prayed that God would use you in great and wonderful ways? Have you dreamed of accomplishing something adventuresome, historic, and life-changing in your family, church, neighborhood, business, or nation?

You have the call of God on your life, too!

You may be an Abraham, who charts a walk of faith for others to follow. You may be a Joseph, who is raised up by God to provide financially and materially for the work of God. You may be an Elijah, who is called of God to minister in extremely difficult situations.

You may be like one of the disciples, not naturally gifted or educated, but called and, therefore, filled with God's ability to tackle the impossible and change the world. You may even be an Apostle Paul, called to move out of your own comfort zone to minister where no one else has ever laid a foundation, or to bring heavenly revelation to those who are spiritually famished.

Maybe God is calling you to be a better businessman, to push far beyond where you currently are into bigger and broader dreams. Perhaps He is calling you to be a more excellent student, pastor, educator, or worker. Is your heart being tugged to excel as a husband, father, wife, mother, son, or daughter, to be more wise and more dedicated to those you love and serve than you have ever been before?

It doesn't matter where you are in life or what you are doing, one thing is sure: you can be more than you are right now.

Your abilities in Jesus Christ are massive, but they will remain unrealized if you do not listen to His voice and follow His plan for your life. With the power of the Holy

Spirit working in you, an exciting life is in your future! No one who truly obeys God is ever bored!

Your time to move ahead is just in front of you. You may be hearing God's voice speaking to you right now as you read this book! Your point of no return may be starting at this very moment.

I'm not certain many believers ever experience the point of no return, primarily because of the personal cost, but also because it is frightening to continuously depend upon the miraculous power of God! But I do know that each time I'm called to press on past the point of no return, I have turned to the Bible for inspiration, wisdom, and courage.

Joshua, who is the subject of this book, has been one of my favorite heros of the faith. He bravely faced the point of no return when Moses died and suddenly, it was his turn to lead the nation of Israel. He would follow in the footsteps of a legend, leading an often rebellious and difficult people into the Promised Land, a land filled with milk and honey — and deadly giants.

This is where we will begin in Chapter Two! Make sure you read carefully and let the Holy Spirit speak to your heart about your own life.

An adventure of faith awaits you!

Chapter Two
It's Time to Move Ahead

Every man or woman who has ever seriously served the Lord — Old Testament, New Testament, and throughout human history — has come to moments in their lives when they faced the point of no return. One of the most powerful and detailed examples the Holy Spirit has given believers is found in the Old Testament, in the life of Joshua.

Joshua had served in the shadow of Moses for decades, just waiting for the time when he would become the leader of the people of God. He supported Moses through the struggle with Pharaoh in Egypt, followed him through the Red Sea, traversed the desert with him for forty years in the wilderness, and stood beside him on countless occasions of trouble among the people of Israel.

Finally, Joshua's moment arrived. What qualities of character caused Joshua to step over the line in faith and pass the point of no return? What are the marks of a true, godly leader?

A Terrible Crisis Births New Greatness

The book of Joshua begins by saying, *"Now after the death of Moses the servant of the Lord it came to pass, that the Lord spake unto Joshua, the son of Nun, Moses' minister"* (Joshua 1:1).

The writer of Joshua begins this book with a grim reminder that a terrible tragedy has happened to Israel. Moses has died. In actual fact, *"Now after the death of Moses"*

19

is the title of the book which we call the Book of Joshua. "Joshua" is an abbreviation, but the real title is the very first phrase of the book.

The title itself, then, indicates that a crisis was taking place in the nation of Israel. Their leader, the venerated and revered Moses, was dead, and they didn't know how they could go any further in God without him. To make matters worse, God had taken the body of Moses and hidden it somewhere in the desert so the Israelites could not find it.

One day, as I was studying and pondering this, it occurred to me why God had hidden Moses' dead body from the children of Israel. Had they known where it lay, they would have built a magnificent tomb around it, set a guard to watch over it, and probably would have stopped in their walk of faith and camped around their dead leader. They probably would have built the "City of Moses" and ceased to go into the land God had promised them.

Moses represented a glorious era of God's power, and it seems when most moves of the Spirit come to an end, people have a hard time letting go of the past, especially those who were part of the era from the very beginning. Rather than move on with the Spirit of God, they are tempted to try to preserve the former time. Though often unintentionally, people stay behind, camping on wonderful, but lifeless and powerless memories. As a result, they miss the next outpouring of God's Spirit.

Through Moses, God had worked signs and wonders in the wilderness. He fed millions of people with manna from heaven. He provided water directly from a rock when there was no water. Even so, with all those miracles, the desert was just a temporary dwelling place, not the place where God intended for them to permanently reside. God wanted to give them something better — the Promised Land — a land that flowed with milk and honey.

Because God wanted His people to keep moving forward, He hid Moses' dead body so they could not find it and build a memorial around it. It was right for the people to remember the miracles of God in the wilderness and to respect and hold Moses dear in their hearts. But God did not want the Israelites to stop dead in their tracks and miss what He had planned for them in Canaan.

Not being able to physically bury Moses must have been psychologically devastating to those who followed him. Part of the natural grieving process when someone dies is to see the dead body and to tell that person farewell. Our human nature requires that we come to grips with finality when a person dies. The funeral confronts us with the reality of their being gone from this life, gives us the opportunity to say good-bye, and frees us to leave the past behind and to move on with life.

The people did not have this opportunity when Moses died. Not only had they lost him, but they didn't know where his dead body was located, so they didn't even get to say farewell to their beloved leader. It was like a double loss. Deuteronomy 34:8 says, *"And the children of Israel wept for Moses in the plains of Moab thirty days: so the days of weeping and mourning for Moses were ended."*

The Greatest Prophet of the Old Testament

Everyone knew Moses was a special man of God like no other. Deuteronomy 34:10 says, *"And there arose not a prophet since in Israel like unto Moses, whom the Lord knew face to face."*

Moses' life constituted a very rare piece of history. Born a Hebrew, he was adopted as an infant by Pharoah's daughter and raised as an Egyptian. As an adult, he converted to the Hebrew faith and became the children of Israel's deliverer from Pharoah. He was the only man ever to see God, and he was chosen to receive the laws of God. The life of Moses was uncommonly unique in the history of mankind.

This same Moses was so mightily anointed by God, so bold and courageous, that he defied the power of Egypt with only a rod in his hand, bringing the plagues of God down upon that oppressive nation. Only Moses had the authority to command the waters of the Nile to turn into blood, the sand to turn into lice, to bring locusts that ate the crops of Egypt, and to call fire and hail from the heavens. Only Moses had the God-given authority to command the Red Sea to part. *Only Moses.*

Moses was in a category of minister all his own. He was one of a kind, truly unique and special in both his anointing and the types of miracles God performed through him. Therefore, when he died, it was a terrible tragedy.

Furthermore, Moses had been Israel's contact with God for forty years. If they wanted to say something to God, they sent Moses to speak to Him on their behalf. When God wanted to speak to the people, He spoke to Moses and Moses gave God's message to the people on behalf of God.

Moses represented the presence and voice of God to that nation. He was the prophet of God, the intercessor of the people, and the mediator between God and man. Therefore, when Moses died, they grieved not only because they lost a dear friend and leader, but because they believed they had lost their representation before God.

What would they do without Moses? How would they hear from God? Who would intercede to God on their behalf? Who would deliver them from the next enemy? Moses was God's instrument the last time. Moses was the only one they knew who had such authority to do miracles like parting the Red Sea.

A huge spiritual vacuum had been created because of Moses' death. The people were naturally scared and obsessed with all these questions. This is the setting for the drama that unfolds in the beginning of the Book of Joshua.

Joshua 1:1 continues, *"Now after the death of Moses the servant of the Lord it came to pass, that the Lord spake unto Joshua. . ."*

Joshua was God's choice for leadership!

Your Day Finally Arrives!

Let me ask you the same question I asked you at the opening of Chapter One: "Have you ever earnestly longed and prayed for something so fervently, every cell and fiber of your being waited in anticipation for that thing to happen, and then, suddenly — *it happened!* — and things began moving so fast that you felt like your head was swimming?"

All those years of waiting and all those gruelling hours of training are suddenly called upon in a moment's time, and your faith must rise up to accept a new position in the kingdom of God. There's no time to pray or think about whether or not you should accept this new assignment. You've been praying and thinking and waiting for it for years! This is your time. This is your hour. *Your day has finally arrived!*

That must have been the kind of excitement and anxiety Joshua felt when he realized his hour to lead Israel had finally come. After serving Moses for decades, and being groomed by God to accept this position, *it happened!* In a flash, Moses was gone and Joshua had been promoted to the highest position of leadership in God's plan.

In one instant of time, the spotlight that had been on Moses for an entire generation abruptly shifted from their dead leader and moved across the stage to Joshua. Now he found himself standing in front of several million Jews, who were probably wondering, "Will he ever be the kind of leader Moses was?"

How would you have felt that day, if you had been Joshua? Imagine the pressure he must have felt when he stepped before millions of grieving Israelites who were sure there could never be another leader like Moses. I can nearly hear Joshua's heart pounding as he stood there, looking into the eyes of the multitudes as they stared back at him, each of them thinking, "Can he do it? Can he lead us? Will he be like Moses?"

Moses would be a hard act to follow!

What if Moses had been your pastor? It would be very hard to settle for someone else, wouldn't it? If every time you came to church he was accompanied by a pillar of fire and billows of smoke, it would be a great let-down to lose him, wouldn't it?

Even Joshua must have wondered, "Am I fit for the task?" "Can I do this?" Mixed emotions that shouted, "Go for it!" one second, and asked, "Are you crazy?" the next probably raged through his natural mind over and over. If he was a normal human being like you and me, his spirit was erupting with joy at the chance to be God's leader, while his flesh wanted to put on the brakes and think about it for a few more days!

This was Joshua's point of no return. He couldn't turn back, slow down, or pass the buck to someone else. He had been training and preparing for this moment for years, and now that moment suddenly burst upon him. This was it. His day had finally arrived.

When he stood and looked out onto the masses of people in his new congregation, reality was hitting him hard and fast. Life as he had known it was gone forever, and his degree of commitment was being required to move up to a higher, more intense level.

Life would never be the same again.

Are You Ready for *Your* New Assignment in Life?

When God opens huge doors of opportunity for you, you may ask, "Am I ready for this? Can I handle this kind of responsibility? Am I spiritually mature enough to deal with all that goes along with this kind of position?"

Those are good questions to ask, but very difficult to answer. If God Himself has truly opened the door, then He has obviously counted you faithful enough at this point in your life to handle a new assignment, or the door wouldn't be opening to you. If you don't think you are mature enough to handle it right now, don't worry! You can be sure God will mature you as you go along.

If you wait until you think you're "ready enough" for your next assignment, you'll probably never do anything for the kingdom of God, because you'll probably never really "feel" like you are "ready."

If the door opens and you hear God beckoning you to walk through, then trust His judgment concerning your "readiness." You are not a good judge of yourself anyway! Remember, the Apostle Paul said, *"Yea, I judge not mine own self"* (First Corinthians 4:3). You should judge yourself in matters of discipline, financial responsibility, how you treat others, and so on. But you should never judge yourself "ready" for a new task in the kingdom of God, especially if it is a big one.

If you let your emotions dictate your "readiness," you will probably never do anything worthwhile in life. Most likely, you won't feel good enough, prepared enough, or mature enough to handle that new assignment. When you look at the immensity of what God is putting before you and asking you to do, you'll probably feel very small and ill-equipped to do it.

That's not entirely bad! As long as those feelings of being ill-prepared don't keep you from accepting God's new assignment, they may be very beneficial to you. It is good to realize your dependence upon God as you initiate a major new step in your life. It is when we become cocky and arrogant, so reliant upon ourselves that we forget our need for God's strength, that we can fail.

On the other hand, don't confuse genuine humility with false humility. Real humility is not beating yourself over the head and constantly thinking, "I'm not worthy to do this." Real humility is realizing your inadequacy to do the job, but accepting God's plan and trusting that with God's help you can get it done.

True humility is recognizing who you are without God, and what you can be if you put your trust in Jesus Christ!

The truth of the matter is, naturally speaking, you are not worthy for your new assignment! Big deal — you weren't naturally worthy to receive salvation, either! You weren't naturally worthy to receive the infilling of the Holy Spirit. You weren't naturally worthy to receive healing or answers to prayer. According to Romans 3:20, by your own deeds and actions you are not worthy of anything except eternal damnation!

That, however, did not change the fact that God chose you, saved you, healed you, and has answered your prayers many times. You didn't naturally deserve any of this, but because His work in your life is a work of grace, you received all of it anyway. You are a recipient of God's wonder-working grace!

Because of His grace, you can look realistically at the inadequacies you feel right now and confidently proclaim, *"I can do all things through Christ which strengtheneth me"* (Philippians 4:13). This verse could be translated, *"I can do all things through Christ, Who, with each new day, is flooding me with a brand-new, continuous stream of fresh power."*

This daily inflow of fresh power comes from abiding in a vital relationship with the Lord Jesus Christ! Dependence upon Him in that relationship is the key to receiving the daily infusion of divine strength and wisdom that will enable you to accept and victoriously fulfill God's next assignment for your life.

You may not feel "ready" for your next new assignment from God, but that's all right. *God* thinks you're ready, and He will provide the grace and power to make you ready. He will mature you, and He will equip you for the task. All He wants is to hear your heart say, "yes" to the next exciting phase of life He is placing before you.

The Apostle Paul Faces the Point of No Return

For the Apostle Paul, the point of no return was a very difficult and painful place, but passing it set him on course for a tremendous supernatural ministry. He had faced the point of no return when he was first saved, but later on he faced it again on his way to Corinth for the first time. In his first epistle to the Corinthians, he reveals his state of mind.

Paul writes, *"And I, brethren, when I came to you, came not with excellency of speech or of wisdom, declaring to you the testimony of God. For I determined not to know anything among you, save Jesus Christ, and him crucified. And I was with you in weakness, and in fear, and in much trembling"* (First Corinthians 2:1-3).

In this verse, Paul reveals his spiritual condition when he first came to Corinth. Notice Paul begins verse 3, *"And I was with you. . ."* The word "with" is taken from the Greek word *pros*, which nearly always describes a "face-to-face" situation. Knowing this, the verse could be translated, *"And when I was face to face with you. . ."*

Because Paul uses the word *pros* ("face to face"), we know that he still vividly recalls the first time he saw the saints in Corinth, who at that time were pagans, immersed in the worst sexual debauchery and depravity. By using the word *pros*, we know Paul is reflecting on the time when he and the Corinthians first laid eyes on each other.

Paul's first visit to Corinth came after a very painful period of ministry. He had just been confronted with angry unbelievers in Antioch and Pisidia, who expelled him from their cities. He was nearly stoned to death in Iconium, and had to flee to Lystra to save his life from the angry mobs.

Still angry and perturbed with Paul, unbelieving leaders traveled from Iconium to Lystra to find him. Having found him, they convinced the city to stone him to death, which they did. The only reason Paul survived this ordeal was because faithful Christians circled his dead body and asked God to raise him from the dead (Acts 14:20).

Paul faced a riot and imprisonment in Philippi, he was chased out of the city of Thessalonica by the local Mafia, he was assaulted by angry Jews in Berea, and faced mocking philosophers in Athens. All of this preceded his journey to the city of Corinth, a city famous for sexual perversion and demonic activity.

As Paul walked over the hills toward the city of Corinth, he was thinking about the way things were going in his ministry. Naturally speaking, things were not going too well! He had been stoned, imprisoned, run out of seven different cities, infuriated both Jews and philosophers, and had gotten in terrible trouble for casting a demon out of a well-known fortune-teller, whose boss lost a great source of his income when the demon was no longer present to provide fortunes.

Paul was a highly educated and intelligent man, and his great intellect and debating ability may have been part of his problem. In Antioch and Pisidia, Iconium and Lystra, Thessalonica and Berea, he "argued" and "reasoned" with the Jews, which is what reaped most of his opposition in these places. As his powerful mind took on either pagan Jew or Greek, "arguing" and "reasoning" with them, he made them so angry that they wanted to kill him!

Headed toward Corinth, Paul was, no doubt, reflecting on his past difficulties and wondering what kind of trouble he would drum up next. One thing had become very obvious, ministering from his own natural ability was not bringing a lot of good fruit! Maybe it was time to let the Holy Spirit take over completely.

Paul made a decision at this point in his ministry to come to a place of absolute surrender to the Holy Spirit's power. This decision was his point of no return. There would be no recourse and no turning back from this new commitment. He told the Corinthians, *"And I, brethren, when I came to you, came not with excellency of speech or of wisdom, declaring unto you the testimony of God. For I determined not to know anything among you, save Jesus Christ and him crucified"* (First Corinthians 2:1,2).

Paul decided to turn from himself, his own abilities, thinking, and excellency of speech. He turned from human wisdom, from debating, reasoning, and arguing, and chose to simply preach *Jesus Christ and Him crucified* from that moment onward. No more superlative preaching from this man of God, just the pure gospel in its simplest form.

It sounds like a simple decision, and it may have been a simple decision for a simple person, but not for Paul! He was a complicated intellectual with great natural ability. Deciding to deny his own persuasive abilities and keep his mind quiet in order to preach a simple message, with no arguing or debating, was a monumental decision for him. Nevertheless, that was the commitment he made out on those hills, as he walked toward Corinth.

Unfortunately, making life-changing decisions are easy when you are home alone in your prayer closet, or walking over the hilltops with no one else around. *The hard reality of these decisions hits us when we leave our prayer closets and private places to deal with life.* That's when our decisions must be carried out — and we find out whether or not we were really serious about them!

It's like laying in bed at night, and saying, "Tomorrow I'm going to start a new diet." When tomorrow rolls around and your friends invite you over for a big, juicy hamburger with lots of wonderful, greasy french fries, you'll face your point of no return head on! That's when you find out if you were serious the night before.

Paul made his decision while on his way to Corinth, but when he arrived and his first public meeting began, he saw all of those faces glaring back into his, and he suddenly became aware of the seriousness of his choice.

In the past, he could have easily resorted to his natural persuasive powers, rhetorical abilities, and intellectual greatness. But now, because he had made a commitment to the Lord and was serious about carrying it out, he could not. He could not speak to them with *excellency of speech or of wisdom, declaring unto them the testimony of God nor to know anything among them, save Jesus Christ and him crucified.*

Therefore, when he found himself face to face with the Corinthians, he later wrote to them, *"And I was with you in weakness, and in fear, and in much trembling."*

Again, the word "with" is taken from the Greek word *pros* and it can be translated "face to face." It is almost as though Paul says, *"And when I was with you, staring into your faces and you were staring back at me..."* He is describing what he felt at that critical moment — his point of no return.

Making a decision out in the countryside was easy for Paul to do, but now, as he looked into their faces, he knew if God didn't do something wonderful soon, he was in trouble! He felt a new helplessness and utter dependence upon the power of the Holy Spirit. Most likely, he was tempted to lapse back into his previous mode of ministry, but he could not do that, because he had crossed the point of no return.

Weakness, Fear, and Much Trembling

Paul continued to say, *"And I was with you in weakness, and in fear, and in much trembling."* This kind of statement would put you in the category of "lack of faith" in many charismatic circles today. But in fact, this *"weakness, fear and much trembling"* was the very attitude that launched Paul into a powerful ministry of faith!

Weakness, fear, and much trembling may not sound like the characteristics of a man of faith and power, but these are the true characteristics of people of faith. It sounds like a contradiction, but it is not, and I will explain.

I know men and women of faith all over the world. They have mountain-moving faith and watch God perform wonder after wonder, yet naturally speaking, they have to deal with weakness, fear, and much trembling every time they stand up to minister. Even as they operate in this miraculous realm of faith that amazes others, weakness, fear and much trembling is what they are feeling. No one else may realize it, because they appear to be so bold and courageous at the moment, but that is what they are most often feeling.

Let me give you an example of what I mean. A preacher steps onto the stage to minister to thousands of people who are sick. He is fully aware that many of them have driven or flown hundreds or thousands of miles to come to his healing service. They are expecting to receive their healing that very night, and that minister is their point of contact to receive a miracle from God. This awareness creates an overwhelming and even desperate feeling of responsibility — like "weakness, fear and much trembling" — in the soul of that preacher!

When that minister looks out into the crowd and sees the great needs, the expectation of the masses, knowing some will die if they are not healed that night, knowing only God can meet every need, heal those sick bodies, and mend every heart — he knows that if the Holy Spirit does not move in that meeting in a powerful way, many people will return home sad, disappointed, and still sick. Knowing that only God can do these miracles creates an utter dependence upon the Holy Spirit.

When God tells you to do something, it will always be a big leap of faith!

Rarely do you have the comfort of doing something small in your own eyes for God. When He speaks, even if it looks small to someone else, you will think He is asking you to take the biggest leap you have ever taken in your life.

When Denise and I first went on the road to teach the Word of God across the United States, we had five meetings booked over a period of two months. We were amazed we even had five, actually! Everybody at home told us we would go broke on the road, that five meetings would never cover two months of expenses and all that travel. But we knew the Lord had spoken to us to go.

We set out and had five glorious meetings! It was a giant step of faith for us, but we did not have a choice, because God had spoken and the mantle was on us to go. As it turned out, those five meetings laid a foundation for our ministry which eventually brought us over nine hundred invitations a year!

Another time, while I was praying in the middle of a worship service, the Lord spoke to me and said, "Son, I want you to send 25,000 of your teaching tapes to missionaries around the world. They are starving for My Word."

I said, "Lord, do you know what that will cost?"

He said, "Take the big leap, and I will provide for you." We sent out the 25,000 tapes, and He provided the funds to do it, but I had weakness, fear, and much trembling going through with it!

When your next new assignment begins, perhaps your next job, your next pastorate, your next school year, or your next project, and you realize you've stepped into something huge, much bigger than you had imagined, and you realize the success of that whole project rises and falls on *your* shoulders, you might feel a little "weakness, fear and much trembling" too. Knowing that you absolutely cannot make a mistake this time will probably cause you to feel a deep need for Someone bigger than you to step in to assist you to get the job done!

As long as we think we can handle something by ourselves, we will be limited to our own ability. But when we realize that our new assignment in life is just too big to handle by ourselves, then we have no choice but to move beyond ourselves and into another dimension — into the dimension of God Himself.

We know from the Book of Acts and church history that Paul had great success in ministry at Corinth. Many were saved and filled with the Holy Spirit. Although they had great difficulty coming out of the lifestyle of sin and debauchery they had known for so long, the hallmark of the Corinthian Church became the supernatural power of the Holy Spirit moving in their midst every time they came together.

Like Paul when he walked into Corinth, Joshua faced the nation of Israel for the first time with the same feelings of weakness, fear, and much trembling. Just the knowledge that he was following in the footsteps of Moses was enough to make him turn and run for the hills! But, also like Paul, he had made a commitment to the Lord, and it was time to move ahead. This is the mark of a great man of God and a great leader.

We Are All Called to Lead

You may be reading this and thinking to yourself, "I'm not called to be a five-fold minister in the Church or the president of my company or anything like that. What has all this leadership stuff got to do with me?"

I challenge you to examine your life, and you will see areas where you are called to lead. If you are a husband, the Bible says you are the head of the marriage (Ephesians 5:23). If you are a wife, the Bible says you are to train and teach your children (Proverbs 22:6). And most important, God has called all of us to make disciples of other believers (Matthew 28:18-20).

I guarantee you, there are some areas of your life where you are called to be a leader, and other areas of your life where you are called to follow, but whether you are a leader or a follower, *in Christ you are always a servant.*

Therefore, when I refer to "leadership" in this book, I am not necessarily referring to being in full-time ministry in the Body of Christ or being President of the United States! You can apply the practical, common sense and wisdom in this book to any walk of life in which you find yourself. Fathers and mothers must lead, older children lead younger children, employers lead employees who lead other employees.

We all find ourselves on the chain of authority, and submission is the name of the game! No matter who you are leading, there is always someone who is in authority over you. Ultimately, your authority is the Lord Jesus Christ!

Following in the Footsteps of Another Leader

Before closing this chapter, I want to address an issue that many of us face when God promotes us: the challenge of following in the steps of another leader.

If your predecessor was a bad leader — immoral, unethical, or lacking honesty and integrity — you will have the challenge of winning the people's trust and respect. This just takes time and patience and perseverence.

Ironically, if your predecessor was a good leader with a long tenure, your road will probably be *more* difficult, and sometimes painful. Because the people have prospered and been happy under the previous leader, they will be very resistant to change, unwilling to adjust to your personality and manner of doing things.

Even worse, what if the previous leader was Moses! Naturally speaking, who would want to try to fill those shoes? Moses had been Israel's pastor, prophet, leader, and beloved friend for forty years. Not only that, he was known to have God's ear and move in God's power. Whether they liked Moses or not, the Israelites who had not perished in the wilderness could not dispute his God-given position and authority.

To complicate matters more, when someone dies, their friends and loved ones can quickly forget all the bad times and all their faults and weaknesses. Israel probably began to exaggerate Moses' good qualities and strengths, turning him into a semi-god within days of his death, saying things like, "There will never be another Moses. I don't know how we can go on without him. No one will ever walk in the anointing Moses walked in or do the miracles he did."

If there was ever a time for feeling inadequate and incapable, it was when Joshua faced the Hebrew nation for the first time. But we must remember, *anyone* who serves God will face this kind of situation, whether a businessman who is promoted to become head of a thriving, successful division of a corporation, or a minister who is called to a church where the beloved pastor of many years has just retired or passed away.

It is interesting that when a church has had one pastor for many years and that pastor retires or dies, it is very common for the next pastor to have a very short term there. The new pastor may be terrific and even better equipped than the old one, but because the church is accustomed to another leadership style, it will be hard for them to make the necessary adjustments to move on quickly.

The bottom line is that the new pastor is not *like* the other pastor. He might be more excellent, moving into higher dimensions of the Word and Spirit, but because he is *different* from the previous pastor, he may not be received well — or at all.

Change is always threatening to people, and new leadership represents change.

When a new pastor is called to a church, the members may make every effort to be open minded, accepting, and gracious. But when the new leader steps into the pulpit to preach for the first month or so, whether consciously or unconsciously, it is normal for people to compare the new pastor with the old one. That is why it is common for a church to go through two or three pastors before they settle down with a pastor who sticks it out and forms his own ministry among them. This is simply symptomatic of human nature.

This is also true of the business world and political world. New leaders, whether new presidents or new employers, are always compared to their predecessors. It is the nature of human beings to watch, compare, talk, test, and try new leadership. This is one reason why following in the steps of a strong leader can be a challenging and often frustrating experience.

How many times have you heard someone say, "Our other boss didn't do it that way! I don't know why we have to change. We've always done it this way, and it's always worked."

Nevertheless — God uses this situation to change everyone's heart.

During this time, if the congregation is sensitive and honest with God, they will acknowledge they are stuck in a rut and need to be more flexible and open to change. Simultaneously, the leadership skills of the new pastor are also revealed.

This time of trial and testing ultimately makes it clear whether or not the new pastor has the anointing and guts to lead that local church into the future. If he does, it will also show clearly which church members were at the church because they liked God's *man*, and which ones are there because God called them there to grow and serve, *no matter who the leader may be.*

If God is calling you to a new assignment in life and a new position of leadership, be realistic about the challenges that go along with your new task. You will be compared to the last leader, questioned as to why you want to do things differently, and may be misunderstood simply because your personality is different from your predecessor.

Remember, that's just human nature! If you've got the guts to face all of that and to keep moving ahead, you'll show them that you're serious, that you're really called by God, and that you truly care about them. Most important of all, as you persevere in faith, God will give you supernatural favor with them. Eventually, they'll buckle-up and follow you just as ardently as they followed the last leader.

Chapter Three
If You Were God, Would You Choose Someone Like You for Leadership?

If you were God, would you choose someone like you for leadership? If you were God and you were looking for leaders, what would you look for? What would be the main characteristics of leadership that caught your attention? What causes God to bring some people into positions of leadership, and not others?

To answer these questions, we must look further at Joshua 1:1. *"Now after the death of Moses the servant of the Lord it came to pass, that the Lord spake unto Joshua, the son of Nun, Moses' minister, saying. . ."* I want you to particularly notice the last part of the verse. It says, *"The Lord spake unto Joshua, the son of Nun, Moses' **minister**. . ."*

Here is a tremendous key to why God chose Joshua: *he was Moses' minister.* One translation says, *"The Lord spake unto Joshua, the son of Nun, Moses' associate. . ."* Some other translations say, *"Moses' assistant, Moses' disciple, Moses' servant,"* and *"Moses' slave."*

One of the marks of a great leader is their willingness and faithfulness to follow those who are in authority.

There is one thing of which we can be sure: when God chose Joshua to replace Moses, he wasn't choosing an unknown, mysterious figure. Joshua had been around a long time and had a proven track record. He had been Moses' associate, assistant, disciple, and servant. He had faithfully served Moses over many years.

Joshua probably did menial and unnoticed tasks, and he may have even felt used and abused by Moses from time to time. Moses was a busy man with many responsibilities, and as his associate, like most associates, Joshua probably did a lot of dirty work and got very little glory. But that's not necessarily bad. This period of serving is a time of testing, which proves whether or not the associate has what it takes to lead.

If they can't follow, then they are not ready to lead.

Furthermore, when you serve in an associate position and have to deal with your fleshly feelings of neglect and being unappreciated by others, God deals with right and wrong motives in your heart. You find out why you are *really* serving the Lord.

Do you serve Him to get glory in the eyes of others, or are you purely serving Him in your current capacity because this is what God has asked you to do? One of the most important things for any associate to discover is the condition of their heart and, unfortunately, serving without gaining any recognition is the best way.

Moreover, in all these challenges, the Holy Spirit encourages you and teaches you to develop a humble heart and mind. Leaders who have learned how to maintain an attitude of humility can make many, many mistakes, but because their heart is right toward God and toward others, He will see them through every calamity or obstacle. While instructing them in their error, He will give them the grace and favor to continue and succeed.

Just think of all the mistakes King David made, but the Book of Psalms tells us that he maintained an attitude of humility through the years. This humility gave David a stature of greatness that exceeded all the other kings of Israel.

Peter admonished us, *"Likewise, ye younger, submit yourselves unto the elder. Yea, all of you be subject one to another, and be clothed with humility: for God resisteth the proud, and giveth grace to the humble"* (First Peter 5:5).

Submitting to authority is always a big test, and a vital one for any leader. It might be that, from time to time, you are tempted to think you've been asked to do something too basic and too menial for someone as greatly anointed as you. But when Peter wrote, *"be clothed with humility,"* he was recalling the Last Supper with the Lord Jesus, when Jesus Himself, the Lord of all, took off his own garment and stooped down on his knees to wash the feet of the disciples. The Lord of Glory was willing to wash the dirty feet of his disciples just before He died for them.

If Jesus could do this, then we should always make it our aim to "clothe ourselves with humility" and faithfully serve those whom God has called us to serve, whether we think the task is menial or awesome. By "faithfulness" I am not referring to mountain-moving faith to work signs and wonders, but rather faithfulness in relationships and in doing the tasks assigned to us.

Faithfulness is the consistent outward manifestation of a humble heart.

Joshua is an example of someone who proved himself "faithful" through the years. Through the thick and the thin of adversity and various challenges, he stayed in his place beside Moses, helping, assisting, and serving him and the people of God for decades.

In the New Testament, when Paul told Timothy to choose leaders, he told Timothy to select *"faithful men, who shall be able to teach others also"* (Second Timothy 2:2). It is important to note that Paul did not tell Timothy to choose *talented* or *capable* men. Rather, he was to choose *faithful* men for notable positions of leadership in the Church.

In order to know whether or not a man is faithful, he must be tested. The whole idea of faithfulness is passing the tests of time, commitment, faithfulness to relationships, and submission to authority. There must be a multitude of tests and a multitude of challenges to truly establish whether or not a person is faithful.

Only experience with someone over time and through all kinds of circumstances and situations will reveal whether or not they are faithful.

That is precisely why Paul told Timothy, *"Lay hands suddenly on no man"* (First Timothy 5:22). All that glitters is not gold! And everyone who looks good to the eye and sounds right to the ear is not necessarily who you want to serve alongside of you in your ministry or place of business. Remember, the serpent was beautiful and more subtle than any beast of the field, yet Satan used the serpent to destroy the paradise of God (Genesis 3:1).

The Bible tells us that Moses trusted Joshua more and more through the years of their association. In the last chapter of Deuteronomy, the Holy Spirit tells us, *"And Joshua the son of Nun was full of the spirit of wisdom; for Moses had laid his hands upon him. . ."* (Deuteronomy 34:9). Through the laying on of hands, Moses confirmed God's call upon Joshua, but he also acknowledged Joshua's faithfulness.

When Joshua stood looking upon the nation he was to lead into the Promised Land, he had already acquired all of these marks of leadership. He had proven himself faithful, had established an attitude of humility, and was willing to stick it out with this often stubborn, rebellious people.

He had also learned a thing or two from his mentor, Moses — good things and bad things, what to do and what not to do. Whether he agreed with Moses or not, approved of him or not, loved him or not, Joshua served Moses as an able minister without complaint.

Flaws, Imperfections, and Unrealistic Expectations

Learning from a mighty man of God is a two-edged sword. On one side, you have before you a sharp example of someone whom God has chosen to lead His people.

Therefore, you may see an incredible vision brought forth and take form, tremendous miracles, and hear revelation from God's Word expounded in an awesome and powerful, life-transforming way.

On the other side of the sword, which is just as sharp, you have before you an example of a *human being* whom God has chosen to lead His people. When you get close to them, you will begin to see their character, their personality, the way they handle all kinds of situations and react to all kinds of people — and you may not like what you see!

At that point of enlightenment, you will have to choose between the following motivations: "Am I serving this man for approval, to share his glory and reputation, and to advance my own ministry, or am I serving this man as unto the Lord?"

We tend to magnify all of Moses' good points, and that's okay, but think about it for a moment. What do you think it would have been like to work for Moses?

This was the man who brought plagues down on the land of Egypt, who parted the Red Sea, who destroyed Pharaoh and his armies, who stood in the presence of God on the holy mountain, who saw the hind parts of God while God covered him with His own hand. What a story! No one else had all of this on their resume!

On the other hand, this was also the man who had such a strong personality, he wanted to completely control his ministry and do everything himself. The situation got so bad, his father-in-law, Jethro, rebuked him and told him to start delegating authority to other people before it killed him (Exodus 18:13-27).

This was the man who was so impatient with God, that when God instructed him to strike the rock once and the water didn't come out as quickly as he wished, he threw a temper tantrum and struck the rock in anger a second time — defying the order of God. Because of this act of anger and contempt, he was kept from entering the Promised Land (Numbers 20:7-12).

Moreover, Moses was the man who wrote of himself, *"Now the man Moses was very meek, above all the men which were upon the face of the earth"* (Numbers 12:3). What kind of ego does it take to say, "There is no one more meek or humble than me in the whole earth"? You would have to have an unbelievably high opinion of yourself to make such a prideful statement!

While it is true that Moses was the mighty prophet of God, he was also a real human being with real imperfections!

Why do I share this? Because people always seem to have unrealistic expectations of anointed leadership. Because leaders are anointed, people somehow get the idea they are immune from normal living and human behavior. Because they are anointed, that somehow translates that they are exempt from carnality and fleshly reactions.

We need to get a grip on this! *People are people.* While we must respect the call of God upon them and recognize God promoted them into the position they hold, we must also allow them to function as normal human beings. It is a false illusion to believe they live on clouds all day long and do nothing but pray and prophesy. They can never live up to that kind of expectation!

The Apostle Paul was very straightforward about his own humanity, and even tells us about the struggles he faced in his personal life. Finally, so aware of his own human weaknesses and keenly aware of the gift of God that dwelt in the midst of his imperfections, he said, *"We have this treasure in earthen vessels, that the excellency of the power may be of God, and not of us"* (Second Corinthians 4:7).

The word "treasure" comes from the Greek word *theasarus*, and it describes "an inexhaustible supply of riches." By using this word, Paul tells us — almost in amazement — that he has within himself an inexhaustible spiritual treasure! Then he continues to tell us that this "inexhaustible spiritual treasure" resides in an "earthen vessel."

The word "earthen" comes from the word *ostrikinos,* and it describes a material so fragile that, if handled too roughly, it will break and fall to pieces right in your hands. Paul tells us that this "inexhaustible spiritual treasure" lives inside a fragile, breakable vessel. What an astonishing fact, that God would place such riches inside of something as temporal and fragile as us!

Paul was well aware that God's gifts resided in his life. But he was just as aware that his human body was nothing more than an "earthen vessel." This does not minimize the treasure, but rather puts things in proper perspective. While richly anointed and gifted by God, we all still live in earthen vessels that are far from perfect. Hence, we should not be surprised when imperfect vessels occasionally behave imperfectly.

We find human imperfections in Abraham, who often struggled in his walk of faith; in David, who committed adultery and murder; and in the powerful prophet Elijah, who destroyed the prophets of Baal one day and ran in total panic from Jezebel the next day. The Apostle Paul, with all of his great revelations, complained to God that he was tired of being bothered by a thorn in the flesh (Second Corinthians 12:7-9)!

Our behavior may not be perfect, and it may not be the way we want it to be, but it is *human.* Until we see Jesus Christ face-to-face and are completely, permanently changed into His image, we will all still have room for improvement in our faith, lives, and character. I guarantee you, if you were very close to them, you would see flaws and weaknesses in your most admired and respected leaders!

An Important Leadership Test

A big test for you will be to see how you respond to a leader's humanity. In the end, if you judge them for being imperfect, then you are not mature enough to move into leadership yourself. You would be setting yourself up for a terrible fall.

If, however, you do pass this strategic leadership test, you will have passed through one of the most difficult hurdles you'll ever encounter, and you will be on your way to becoming someone God can use powerfully in this world.

When people see a believer who moves in the power of God, they tend to forget they are just a human being. They categorize them as nearly superhuman, and different from average, normal people. That unrealistic expectation will wear off very quickly if they work closely with them, however!

Up close, the blemishes that were never apparent begin popping out, and the devil will use these character faults to try to discourage, disappoint, distract, and deter you from submitting to the man or woman of God you have been called to serve. If you have unrealistic expectations of the person under whom God has placed you, their true personality can be a shock to your system! Ultimately, you will either choose to be offended, or choose to forgive them, pray for them, and serve them in an even more excellent manner.

It is clear that Joshua passed this strategic leadership test. He walked with Moses, worked with Moses, served Moses, and stayed with Moses through all the ups and downs and difficulties of the time they spent together. But personally, I had a tremendous struggle with this test.

Before I started the small church in Arkansas, I served on the staff of a huge Southern Baptist Church. The pastor, in my estimation, was one of the best Bible teachers in the United States. I respected and admired this man because he read Greek, knew Hebrew, and taught the Word of God verse-by-verse like a Bible scholar, but he also believed in the infilling of the Holy Spirit.

Having been reared in the sound doctrines of the Southern Baptist denomination, and then baptized in the

Holy Spirit as a teenager, I had hungered to follow a man of God who brought sound doctrine and supernatural power together in ministry. In my thinking, this was the finest combination desired!

When I first began attending the large church this man pastored, I would sit on the front row every week, nearly hypnotized as he taught the Scripture. "Surely," I thought, "this man's teaching must be similar to the teaching of the Apostle Paul." Everything in my being yearned to know this pastor inside and out, to work with him, assist him, and to serve him. I was willing to do anything to be close to that kind of wisdom and anointing.

Finally, the day came when God opened the door for me to join the staff of this pastor's church. Part of my responsibility was to strengthen a division of the Sunday School that had been weak, and the other part of my job was to do whatever the pastor needed me to do. I was thrilled!

My division of the Sunday School began to grow by leaps and bounds. A national magazine for the Southern Baptist Sunday School Board invited me to write several articles about why my division was growing so rapidly. We began to see scores of people saved and discipled, and our denomination was very interested in the methods we were using to achieve such success so quickly.

Every Monday morning, the pastor held a pastoral staff meeting in his office. I could hardly wait to get there each week to share all my glowing reports of what God was doing in our Sunday School division. I would sit there quietly, listening as the other pastors shared about their own areas of ministry, thinking to myself, "If I were you and that's all I had to share, I would be embarrassed!" I knew that my division was far exceeding theirs!

One Monday morning, I waited for my turn with my usual attitude of critical impatience, until it was finally time for me to share. With great exultation, I reported all the wonderful things that were happening in my division.

When I was finished, I looked at my beloved mentor, fully expecting him to say, "That's wonderful, Rick! You are the greatest, most inspiring member of our team! We are so grateful God has given you to us. Where would we be without you?"

Instead, he looked sternly at me, reached down and took off one of his expensive shoes, and said, "Rick, I scuffed my shoes this morning as I was walking out of the house. I want you to take them to the shoe repair shop right now and have them repaired. The rest of the pastors will stay here and continue our meeting, but as for you, I want you to have my shoes buffed.

"Here are my car keys," he continued. "You can drive my car over to the shoe shop and, while you're out in my car, please wash it, wax it, buff it, and vacuum it before you bring it back. Then when you get back, I'll give you another assignment."

I'll never forget how devastated I felt that day. Rather than hear him say, "Great job!" I heard nothing. In fact, he seemed to ignore me altogether! As I walked out of his office, I thought, "What an ingrate! I'm working my fingers to the bone night and day and all he says is 'now go shine my shoes.' He can't even say 'thank you'!"

That day, I did what every associate is tempted to do from time to time. *I picked up an offense.* When you pick up an offense, suddenly you begin to see things you *never* saw before. Because I was offended, it didn't take too long for me to see *what I wanted to see.* Whereas before he was the most anointed man on earth in my mind, now I began to see him as selfish and self-centered. Day by day my offense got bigger, until I even began to think, "If the rest of the church could see what I see, if they knew him the way that I know him, they wouldn't be so thrilled anymore!"

The truth is, there were some minor flaws in his life, but *very minor.* There are minor flaws in every person's life. Everyone has blind spots that he or she can't see. But because I was offended, those minor and not even worth mentioning blind spots looked huge to me. My offense completely colored my opinion of him and began to tarnish a relationship God desired to be good. I began to think, "Well, if I was the pastor, I'd do this and that differently. If I was the pastor, I'd be more loving. If I was the pastor. . ."

There were times when he could have been more loving, but so could I. There were times when he could have been more grateful, but so could I. And there were times when he was a little hard and insensitive, but they were *very, very rare.*

In reality, my mentor was a man of integrity and good character, but my offended flesh temporarily saw none of these wonderful attributes in his life. Because I held onto my offense, all of his negative traits were magnified in my imagination to an abnormal degree.

I was very wrong, and as I look back on this situation, I thank God it happened! God wisely used this precious man to expose character flaws in me that needed to be dealt with. *Though I thought I was so modest and humble, pride and arrogance were exposed in my own life through this man's careful handling of me.* He knew that if I was going to be used in a significant way in the future, pride had to be broken and dealt with in my life.

He wisely had me shining his shoes and washing his car in the midst of my great achievement. My ugly reaction to him exposed something in me that I didn't know was there. I saw I had to purify the motivations of my heart and the thoughts of my mind. Thank God for that pastor's insight into my life. What he required from me, which I had initially thought was so unjust and unfair, was good!

Looking back on that experience, I am so grateful to God for allowing me to learn under such a good and wise man. Yes, he had minor flaws, but who doesn't? The real problem was my age. I was young, inexperienced, and wanted to be respected and viewed as an equal — but I was not an equal in any way, shape, or form. Where I was just beginning my pilgrimage, this man had walked intimately with God for years.

Eventually, I began to grow up and receive instruction from him. I got close to the man, and after that time of offense had passed, I began to realize all leaders have flaws and idiosyncrasies which are no different from the rest of us. Though leaders, they are normal human beings who need to grow and change, also.

As their servants and associates, we can either stick to our offense and stand in judgment of them — causing a great and possibly insurmountable hindrance to fulfilling our calling — or allow God to mature us by forgiving them, being faithful and obedient to them, and working on our own flaws (Hebrews 12:1).

Passing the Leadership Test

Joshua must have passed this same kind of leadership test. How do we know? Let me ask you again: *What do you think it would be like to work for Moses?*

We've already seen that Moses had a high opinion of himself, that he didn't like to delegate authority to others, and even grew impatient and threw a temper tantrum in the sight of God. If he lost his temper with God, you can count on the fact that he lost his temper with people.

Furthermore, if Moses' judgment was questioned, he could truthfully say he was the only one God had ever known face-to-face, that he knew more about God and His ways than anyone else, and, "Who are you to question me?"

He could truthfully say God used *him* to bring plagues on Egypt, God used *him* to part the Red Sea, God used *him* to destroy Pharaoh's army, God used *him* to deliver the Ten Commandments, and so on. *Can you imagine working for a man with all of those credentials?* What could young Joshua ever tell the spokesman of God that he didn't already know? If anyone was a know-it-all, it would have been Moses.

However, through the years and through every kind of problem, through every imaginable sort of rebellion and insubordination, through negativism and evil reports, through disagreements and even through temper tantrums, Joshua refused to budge from his God-called place beside Moses, faithfully serving, assisting, and helping him in any way required.

Joshua passed the leadership test! He could have become disillusioned with the flaws he saw in Moses' life and left the faith altogether. He could have been bitterly disappointed that the man of God was not always perfect and tried to overthrow him. He could have even written a tell-tale book on the "real" Moses whom other people did not know. But Joshua did none of these things.

As a result, when Moses died and this gaping hole of leadership was created, God did not reach for a newcomer to fill that hole. Rather, He personally elected Joshua, knowing that, because Joshua had learned to submit to a man, and sometimes a very difficult man, he would be able to submit to an invisible God and do whatever God required of him.

If you want to be used by God in a leadership capacity, then do not despise where you are right now.

What you are doing right now may seem small and insignificant, but the actions, attitude, and faithfulness you are developing will become the foundation for your future usefulness to God. Jesus said that if you were faithful over the little things, then He would give you rule over much (Matthew 25:21).

If you are serving in a church and you feel you are in a difficult situation, not being appreciated the way you should be or doing exactly what you feel you are called to do, in the long run you'll see God was *"working in you both to will and to do of his good pleasure"* (Philippians 1:13). While He is working good things into you, He is weeding bad things out of you at the same time. This is an important time in your life — don't despise it! Someday, you will thank God for every moment of it.

A word of caution: If you find you have a critical spirit toward those in leadership over you, then you are not yet ready for a leadership mantle. If your expectations of other leaders are beyond reason, then you must realize God uses real people, just like you. Don't let their humanity send you into disillusionment or despair.

Show mercy now and, someday, when you are placed in an important leadership position, people will show mercy to you in spite of your failures and flaws.

Don't Waste Time!

After dreaming of what it would be like to be Moses for all those years, in one moment's time the spotlight shifted from the now-deceased leader to Joshua — and Joshua became the new Moses! Emotionally, he most likely felt slightly panicked, crying inside, "Oh my gosh, it has finally happened! It's here! It's no longer a dream! What do I do? I'm the new Moses ! ! !"

I know what Joshua wished he could do. He probably wished he could go talk to Moses and get a little advice! But an afternoon session to discuss a few ideas with Moses was an impossible dream. His mentor was dead, and all of the responsibilities were now resting on him.

Joshua stood in front of several million Israelites. Looking at their new leader, they were naturally comparing him to Moses and were probably speculating whether or not he would be able to fill Moses' shoes. He was probably looking back at them, wondering, "Will I ever be able to handle this job?"

All those years of training in Joshua's life were going to be called upon. All that time he spent with Moses and the training for this moment was going to be put into action. It seems that in one second, Moses was gone, and Joshua's life changed.

God was calling Joshua to a new place of commitment. If he was going to obey God with his life and do what God had set before him, it would require him to put aside his fears, his questions, his doubts, and his insecurities in order to move into a higher realm of faith and courage.

Your time will also come! Right now, the Holy Spirit may have you in training for future leadership. All of your experiences and all of the time and energy you are exerting in the present will eventually be called upon in your future. Don't take this time in your life lightly!

If you are serving another leader, a pastor, or an employer, serve them with all of your heart, do the very best job you can do, and let God show you areas of your own heart that need to be changed. If you let God deal with you now, it will spare you sorrow upon sorrow later down the road when you become a leader yourself.

If you are faithful to the call of God upon your life, the day will come when you will see the vision God has given you come to pass. Suddenly, all your dreams will begin happening, and you will have the rock solid knowing that things will never be as they once were.

At that moment, after soundly dealing with all your fears and doubts and questions, with both trepidation and exultation, you will push yourself beyond the line God has asked you to cross. In the knowledge that He has chosen you, molded you, and prepared you, that you have allowed him to make you the kind of leader He needs for the job, *you will pass the point of no return!*

Chapter Four
Focusing on Your Future

When most people are called into full-time ministry, they want to hear a powerful prophetic word to kick their ministry off with a supernatural bang! They fantasize of receiving a prophecy that goes something like, "Yes, I have called you and anointed you to take My Word to the nations," says the Lord.

That's what most ministers would like to hear! Or, "Yes! I have ordained you to preach My Word and to move in the power of My Spirit," says the Lord, "and I will do wonderful and earth-shaking things through your mighty ministry." Those are the kinds of prophetic utterances young new ministers love to hear when they first get started!

But that is not the kind of prophetic word that kicked off Joshua's ministry. He received a word all right, but it wasn't very flowery and it didn't even sound too prophetic. It was straight to the point, hard to hear, and struck him like a slap in the face. God simply said: *"MOSES MY SERVANT IS DEAD!"*

What a way to start your ministry! Yet, that is the way Joshua's ministry began. In Joshua 1:2, God told him, *"Moses my servant is dead: now therefore arise, go over this Jordan, thou, and all this people, unto the land which I do give to them, even to the children of Israel."*

When Joshua heard those fateful words, they must have hit him hard. Mourning for Moses would not help or change the situation, for his role had been fulfilled, and it was time for the next phase of God's plan to be carried out by Joshua. It was time for Joshua to stop looking backward and start looking forward, *focusing on the future.*

Have you ever come to one of those places in your life when you knew that, as glorious and wonderful as your present experience has been, it is finished? When you finish this phase of your spiritual life, you know it can no longer be extended or repeated. As sweet and precious as that period of your life has been, you know it is now time for you to move on toward the next new assignment God gives you.

You don't want to stay where you are anyway! If you stay where you are, never breaking into new territory with your life and with your dreams, then you'll never know what life would have been like living out on the edge! Believe me, when you step out to obey God — whether it is to witness to your neighbor, accept a new position at work, start a new business, go into the ministry, or move across the world to a communist country to preach the gospel — all of it feels like you're living out on the edge!

Then, after you've lived out on the edge for awhile and grown accustomed to the daily adventure of serving Jesus Christ, you'll wonder how you were ever satisfied before. In retrospect, your old life looks gray, boring, and terribly uneventful compared to your new walk of obedience, power, and daily excitement.

Before God called me to take our ministry to the utter-most parts of the earth, I was happy and fulfilled in the United States. As I told you earlier, we had worked very hard to see our ministry grow, and we were seeing great success. When we remembered how we had once lived in that small town in Arkansas, pastoring that little church, we saw how we had stretched and grown in our faith to be able to begin and build a nationwide teaching ministry.

In our view of things, we were really living on the edge then! I never imagined life could have been more fulfilling or exciting. On the other hand, from where we stand right now, living and ministering in the former USSR makes the challenges of the road ministry look pale by comparison!

However, the period of building a nationwide teaching ministry was the very foundation of what we are doing now. It was a necessary phase of spiritual growth and a time to develop relationships God is still using today. To have skipped that period would have been like going from step one to step ten, missing all the vital steps in between. We could not be where we are today without taking all of the other steps to get here.

With all of those steps in place and solid relationships established in the Body of Christ, we could begin our journey to take the Word of God to the uttermost parts of the earth. "Living on the edge" took on a brand new meaning to us. Before, it meant being able to do what God called us to do and pay all of the bills on time. Now, living on the edge means doing all that *plus* going where no one else has gone before, taking God's Word to regions where people have never heard the gospel preached or the Bible taught.

Our faith has grown to such a level that all of this no longer sounds scary, but rather, thrilling. We're like a pack of race horses, just waiting for the Lord to give us our next naturally impossible task, so we can enter the next phase of our spiritual race!

Paying the bills will always be a part of what we're doing, just like it's a part of everyone's life every month. But now, the whole scene has changed, and our perspective is different. Our faith for God to provide is established. Our world vision has expanded. As one dear friend so aptly says, the world has become our playground, the place where God has called us to live and work!

For now, He has called us to take the teaching of His Word to the United States, Europe, and the farthest ends of the former USSR. What will be next? We are more and more focused on the future each day we serve Him. I lie awake in bed at night and dream of taking His Word to Mongolia, China, and other unreached parts of Asia, the war-torn regions of eastern Europe, and the Islamic countries of the Middle East.

The prospect of teaching the Bible on television and in personal speaking engagements in Iran, Iraq, and Turkey absolutely thrills my soul! Yet, years ago this would have terrified me! But frankly, every new step of faith makes the last one look so easy and uneventful. And don't say it's impossible, because we're already doing what no one thought was possible!

Where is your next great leap of faith? Leaving your current job to accept one with greater responsibilities? Biting the bullet, quitting your job and starting the new business you've had in your heart for a long time? Recognizing you've finally met the woman or man God wants you to marry, and finally saying "yes" to marriage? Or, pushing your fears aside to share Christ with your neighbor or unsaved family members?

We are all at different phases and places in our lives. What is important is that you continue to move forward and focus on the future. Don't get bogged down and lose the vision God has given you for your life.

What are you going to do with your life? What is your next step? If you are stuck in a rut, are you going to stay where you are? Or are you going to break out of your stale mode into the adventure that God Almighty has planned for you?

Taking the Big Leap of Faith

If your answer to those questions is, "Yes, I'm willing and ready to move on, and I want to do the will of God with my life," then you need to pay close attention to the next words God spoke to Joshua.

Joshua 1:2 says, *"Moses my servant is dead: now therefore arise, go over this Jordan, thou, and all this people, unto the land which I do give to them, even to the children of Israel."*

Notice God tells Joshua, *"Now therefore arise. . ."* This is an extremely important statement, because God uses the word *NOW*.

You may have heard clearly from the Lord, but you are waiting for the circumstances to be absolutely perfect before you obey. The situation will never be perfect! When God told Joshua to cross the Jordan River, it was at flood stage. Believe me, there was not a more difficult time to begin a ministry than that!

Many use the excuse that they are waiting on the perfect timing of the Lord. But if God has spoken to you and said *NOW*, that is the perfect timing of the Lord! In fact, if the conditions are perfect, you might need to take a closer look and ask the Holy Spirit for discernment.

Perfect conditions do not mean perfect timing.

There comes a time in your life when you don't need to pray about your future any more. Joshua didn't need to stop and say, "Lord, let me pray about this for a few days." He had been praying about this opportunity for many years! His whole life had been spent training for this very moment. Now, when the moment came, only the action of obedience was required of him. That's why God said *NOW*.

Many times people over-spiritualize things, saying, "Let me pray about this, or pray about that," and while they are praying, they miss the golden opportunity God set in front of them. They lost that opportunity because it was the opportunity of the moment. It was a *NOW* opportunity.

There is a time to pray, and there is a time to act. Most believers confuse the two and end up praying a lot, but not doing much with their lives. How can you know when it is time to pray and when it is time to act?

There are two kinds of hesitation. A hesitation in your spirit is the Holy Spirit telling you to slow down, but your own natural hesitation is your flesh not wanting to move forward into something new and unfamiliar. Most often, you will find that it is your own natural hesitation which is speaking to you.

It is very important for you to discern which voice you are listening to, yours or the Holy Spirit's. If it is the Holy Spirit's, then you will have an unshakable, immoveable warning on the inside that you need to stop and pray. If it's your own natural hesitation you are hearing, then you need to shove those fears aside and forge ahead to do what God has told you to do.

If the opportunity before you right now is a door you have kicked open yourself, it's time to stop, pray, and find out where the Holy Spirit wants you to be. Young ministers, businessmen and businesswomen, and even volunteers in the church, will try to manipulate themselves into positions of authority or promote themselves, and this is disastrous!

Let God promote you! If you promote yourself too soon, you will not be prepared to do the job. Follow where He leads you, and pass every test He brings you to with courage and faithfulness. Remember, He's the only one who knows what you need to succeed and when you are ready for that great door of opportunity.

If the opportunity before you right now is the one you've been praying and waiting for, has *supernaturally* opened, and everything looks like God is giving you a green light, then go for it! If you are nervous about it, that's normal! You are about to do something you've never done before. Don't allow that natural edginess to keep you from something wonderful. Those steps of faith only look huge because you have never taken them before.

Once you step out into the realm of faith to accept this new place to which God is calling you, you'll realize it wasn't so hard after all. If this is what you've been praying for, recognize God is working and stop over-spiritualizing things! Over-spiritualizing can rob you of God's blessings when they try to come to you.

When we first began broadcasting our television program in the former Soviet Union, I was visiting with a very powerful communist leader. He looked at me and said, "Rick, can you please provide us with a quality music television program for young people that has strong Christian moral lyrics?" I remember thinking to myself, "Should I pray about this before I answer?"

The answer came loud and clear to my spirit! "When a door swings open, and it is opened by an atheist who has been taught to resist the gospel, and now he is asking you to provide Christian music for atheistic young people to hear, you don't stop to pray about it. You simply say 'Yes!'"

I could have said, "Let me think about it awhile," and gone home to pray for several weeks before I answered him. But who knows what would have happened in that time? By the next time I saw that communist leader, his heart may have changed and I would have lost an opportunity to take the gospel to young people all over Russia. That was a *NOW* opportunity. Thank God, we recognized God was opening a door and accepted the challenge!

The important thing is to obey when you know God is calling you to accept a new assignment in life. If the door is opened, why not go ahead and walk through it? Ultimately, someone is going to do what God has called you to do, and it might as well be you!

What opportunity is before you right now? Are your circumstances lining up for you to fulfill the dream that has been in your heart? Does it look like you have a green light to move forward? Then go for it! This may be your *NOW* opportunity. Don't let this opportunity pass by you and then leave you wondering what would have happened had you taken the big leap of faith! Take the leap!

Preparation, Not Perfection

God continued to tell Joshua, *"Moses my servant is dead: now therefore arise. . ."* I want you to especially notice that God tells Joshua, *"ARISE. . ."*

It was Joshua's time to be promoted in the kingdom of God. He could not hesitate, waver, or allow any of his own insecurities to stop him now. This was his time to rise to the challenge and move forward into God's plan for his life. It was time for Joshua to *ARISE!*

One translation uses the word "prepare" instead of "arise." The person God uses is someone who prepares. They listen to hear the voice of God in prayer and break the bread of life to understand and do the Word. They do not sit around, twiddling their thumbs, waiting for their ministry to begin. They learn all they can learn, soaking up everything the Holy Spirit teaches them, year after year after year.

Joshua was a man of preparation. He watched Moses, imitated Moses, was discipled by Moses, and did all that was necessary to get himself ready for the moment when God would call upon him. Joshua's promotion did not happen overnight! He spent decades preparing for the time when he would become the leader of the nation of Israel.

I often hear people say about others, "Wow! That guy's ministry has really skyrocketed fast, hasn't it?" Or, "Isn't it amazing how quickly her ministry has gained national prominence?" However, when you really get to know these people whom everyone seems to think are instant successes, you find out there is absolutely nothing instant about their success.

Most of them have been around a long, long time and have been working hard at their ministries for years. It just so happens that the fruit of their hard labors has recently come to blossom and to be recognized. There are few quick successes, but the ones who do achieve success instantly usually don't last very long, because they haven't achieved the maturity necessary to maintain success.

This is true in the business world as well. People are generally unknown until they are placed in a highly visible position. When they have never had a visible position before, no one knows who they are. They've been there, working hard all along, but now, because they have been thrust into a more prominent position, everyone sees them and hears about them. This is often when people say, "How in the world was he promoted so fast? Where did she come from anyway?" In reality, it wasn't a quick promotion at all!

This kind of promotion comes after years of learning submission, faithfulness, and hard work. The new visible leader, whom everyone thinks has just stepped into their new role of authority from nowhere, came up through the ranks from the basement, where he or she had their first job in the company. After years of diligence, they've reached a new height which they have earned through the sweat of their brow!

It may have appeared to some that Joshua stepped onto center stage from nowhere. A few probably thought he was one of those incredible overnight success stories. But when you look closely at Joshua's life, you find out he had been around for a long, long time before he was promoted into a highly visible position.

Forty years earlier, when Moses was sending his first delegation of spies to search out the Promised Land, Joshua was among them. At this time, when Joshua was generally unknown to the people of God at large, Moses recognized Joshua's faithfulness. He knew he could depend on Joshua to undertake this critical mission of espionage.

When that first delegation of spies returned home from the Promised Land, all but two declared the land was much too difficult to take. Joshua and Caleb were the two who disagreed. Joshua was full of faith when he said, *"If the Lord delight in us, then he will bring us into this land, and give it us"* (Numbers 14:8). His spirit was right, and he was willing to do whatever was necessary to accomplish the task in front of them.

Therefore, to say Joshua was an instant success would be a great miscalculation. We've already seen how he had been working alongside of Moses for years before the spotlight shifted and came to rest on him. His success only appeared to be sudden because he had been serving in the shadow of Moses most of that time.

When Moses died, the shadow Joshua had been working behind vanished, leaving Joshua standing in the light. *He had been standing there all the time, but was hidden in the shadow.* He was a hard working, faithful servant who had been living and learning in the corridors of leadership and servanthood for several decades. His debut came after years of training and preparation.

Don't be discouraged if it takes a long time for you to move into a prominent position in your ministry or in your business! Don't let tales of instant successes discourage you. If you dig very deep into the heart of those instant success stories, you will most often find that they weren't instant at all. They took a lot of work and sweat, prayer, faith, and believing God to get where they are. They started out just like you did, and they had to face the same devils you may be facing right now.

The ingredient that usually brings prominence is not tremendous gifts, talents, or abilities, but rather a stick-with-it attitude and determination to keep going even when the going gets tough. Remember, Jesus had to face the cross in order to reach resurrection, and the cross was no joy ride!

Taking Jesus as Our Example

Hebrews 12:2 tells us to look at the Lord to see what he endured to finish His race. *"Looking unto Jesus the author and finisher of our faith; who for the joy that was set before him endured the cross, despising the shame, and is set down at the right hand of the throne of God."*

Jesus is the author and finisher of our faith, yet His walk of faith took Him to a cross and to a death. These were necessary phases of His faith walk if He was going to accomplish the assignment God the Father had given to Him. His job was to redeem mankind, and in order to do that, His death was required.

The Lord Jesus clearly did not enjoy the cross! As a matter of fact, Hebrews 12:2 says He *endured* the cross and *despised* the shame. Would you want to be scourged, ridiculed, stripped naked, beaten horribly, and ultimately crucified before the whole mocking world? Would you want to spend three days in the darkness of hell? Of course you wouldn't!

Jesus didn't want to do it either, but because He had His sight set on us being redeemed, because He had His sight set on being seated at the Father's right hand, *because He was focused on the future,* He endured all of it, and he accomplished what the Father sent Him to do! (For more Greek exegetical teaching on Hebrews 12:2, see my book *Living in the Combat Zone,* pages 225-227).

Jesus could have called ten thousand angels to deliver Him from this difficult moment. He could have said, "Father, I've decided that I don't want to go through with this." However, because He had His heart set on redeeming you and me, He endured the suffering, and through His death procured reconciliation between God and man!

Jesus' creature comforts were not as important as the task the Father had given him. If His temporary comforts had been that important, He wouldn't have been born in a manger stall. He wouldn't have grown up in Nazareth, and He wouldn't have faced the cross. Doing what He was sent to do was foremost and paramount in His heart and mind.

Likewise, you've got to be committed if you are going to become all God wants you to be. Those who are more concerned about their creature comforts than achieving victory will eventually fall by the wayside. But if you are willing to pay the price, when all those pushovers are gone, you'll be standing tall and win the prize! Through endurance and faith, you will have proven yourself a mighty champion of faith.

In that day, you'll know better than anyone else that your faith may not always have been as strong as everyone thought! Your faith may have been extremely rocky from time to time. But because you had the guts to stay in the fight and never give up, never losing sight of what God called you to do, people will say you were a spiritual giant!

The mixture of courage, guts, and determination is a formula that always produces people of prominence, those who stand taller than anyone else. Because they were willing to go the distance, their persevering attitude and drive eventually produced greatness in their lives!

Let Your Roots Grow Down
Deep to Give You a Sure Standing

Before a fruit-producing tree reaches a time in its growth when it blossoms and bears fruit, it first must send its roots down deep into the earth, where it can draw a constant source of nourishment. While it is being nourished from below, it begins to send its limbs upward and outward.

The tree endures the heat, the cold, the sleet, the rain, the snow, and all of the seasons before it ever blossoms. Because those roots are tapped into a continuous source of strength, nourishment, and energy, the tree is able to outlast all the seasons and eventually become fruit producing.

Psalm 1:3 says that the man or woman who is rooted in God's Word is *like a tree planted by the rivers of water, that bringeth forth his fruit in his season; his leaf also shall not wither; and whatsoever he doeth shall prosper.*

If you are wondering how long it is going to take before your fruit-producing season finally arrives, don't get too discouraged. The bigger the tree, the greater the need for time to send its roots down deep into the earth to draw nourishment and to give it a firm footing against wind, weather, and pestilence.

Take this time to send your roots down deep and tap into the strength of God's Word and God's Spirit. If your roots are securely fixed into Jesus Christ, you will outlast every season, every foul climate, and every storm. Eventually, you will enter into the fruit-producing season of your life, your ministry, your family, or your business.

Paul wrote to the church at Colossae, *"Let your roots grow down deep into him and draw your nourishment from him. See that you keep on growing in the Lord, and become strong and vigorous in the truths you were taught"* (Colossians 2:7, TLB).

Thank God your promotion has not come quickly, for you would not have had the root, the depth, and the sure foundation to bear you up through the difficulties you will face when the mantle of leadership is passed onto you.

Work on your own personal life, your mind, your thinking, your discipline, your finances, your weight, your relationships, and your behavior. While you are waiting for the promotion that your heart is so set on, use this time of your life to put off the old man and to put on the new man (Colossians 3:9-10).

Spend this phase of your life wisely by renewing your mind to the Word of God (Ephesians 4:23) and being certain your affections are set on things above, not on things on the earth (Colossians 3:2). If you have all of these things in line in your life, you will be in good shape for leadership when the moment of your promotion comes.

One of the saddest things I've seen in the Body of Christ is talented men and women who are promoted too quickly, and therefore, do not have the root, the depth, and the character to sustain them. How many times have you heard about a celebrity or some other famous person who has gotten saved, and then within weeks or a few months of their salvation, they are already preaching?

Those people often start with a big bang, but they end as a terrible fizzle. Those who promoted them so quickly did them a great injustice. They should have encouraged their new converts to get involved in a local church, hearing and beginning to do the Word of God, and being discipled until maturity began to develop in them. Then, when they were ready, God Himself would speak to them and they would be ready to be sent out.

Let what you see in your future be the motivation to get yourself straightened out and grow to maturity in the present!

Time to Prepare, Grow, Change, and Become Trusted

The Apostle Paul was a naturally talented and gifted man. Even before he met Jesus Christ, he was well-known and respected in important Jewish circles. He was from the tribe of Benjamin, a member of the Sanhedrin, and was a nationalistic extremist for the cause of Israel. Because of his education, he had become one of the greatest intellectual minds of his time.

When Paul accepted Jesus Christ as his Messiah, it should not surprise us that he thought, if anyone deserved to be a leader of the Christian community, it should be him! He was saved one day, and almost the next day he was in the City of Jerusalem, trying to make his way into the circle of believers. He was still so new to the faith, they weren't even sure if he was really saved!

Acts 9:26-27 says, *"And when Saul (that's Paul) came to Jerusalem, he assayed to join himself to the disciples: but they were all afraid of him, and believed not that he was a disciple. But Barnabas took him, and brought him to the apostles, and declared unto them how he had seen the Lord in the way, and that he had spoken to him, and how he had preached boldly at Damascus in the name of Jesus."*

Barnabas believed Paul's testimony, but the disciples did not send out advertisements that the world's greatest Christian killer had been saved, nor did they immediately launch him into an itinerant ministry to reach the world for Jesus. They were wiser than that!

Instead, Paul was put on a ship and sent back to Tarsus, his own home town. There, he probably shared the news of his salvation with his family and took care of any personal business that needed attention. What happened with his family no one can say for sure. But one thing is certain! Paul's public ministry didn't begin until nearly thirteen years after his salvation experience!

In those thirteen years, Paul served God and the members of the apostolic team who were nestled in Antioch. He studied the Bible, gained new and incredible insights into the Lord Jesus from the Old Testament, and began to mature in his character.

Finally, it was time for him to be sent out onto the mission field, but even then he was not sent out alone. He traveled with Barnabas, the man who first brought him to the apostles in Jerusalem and had taken spiritual oversight of him as he was growing in his walk with the Lord.

This is why Paul is able to tell us, *"Lay hands suddenly on no man"* (First Timothy 5:22), and do not use a novice or new believer, because they aren't ready for leadership yet (see First Timothy 3:6). This is why Paul demands that elders and deacons be men of character who have already proven their sincerity and stability in the local church before they are promoted into visible positions of leadership (First Timothy 3:1-13). He was actually speaking from personal experience!

Concerning himself, Paul told the Thessalonians, *"But as we were allowed of God to be put in trust with the gospel, even so we speak; not as pleasing men, but God, which trieth our hearts"* (First Thessalonians 2:4). I want you to notice the first part of the verse which says, *"But as we were **allowed** of God. . ."*

"Allowed" is taken from the Greek word *dokimadzo*. Historically, this word was used to depict a man who had undergone many rigorous tests and trials to determine whether or not he had enough character to be placed into a position of leadership. If he could not pass a number of character tests over a period of time, then he was deemed unfit for public service and eliminated from ever being used in that way. Strength of character was more important than gifts or talents!

Therefore, when Paul says, *"But as we were allowed of God,"* he is making a powerful statement to us about his own walk with the Lord. Rather than being thrust into a position of leadership quickly after his new birth, he had been put through a myriad of grueling character tests which would prove him fit or unfit for leadership in the kingdom of God. Though he was called to the ministry, God would not allow him to move into a visible position of leadership in the Body of Christ until his strength of character had been developed, tested, and shown trustworthy.

Most likely, part of the process of gaining maturity was learning to sit quietly and listen to the more spiritually mature men of Antioch, perhaps less educated than himself, but more knowledgeable and experienced in spiritual matters. He was also learning to serve in unnoticed ways, which he may have thought were far below his abilities and an insult to his intelligence, learning to simply be a brother like everyone else.

Promotion did not come quickly for Paul. Thirteen years later, after a lot of dealing with his flesh, pride, and strong will, God finally deemed him fit to enter the full-time ministry. In Acts, chapter thirteen, Paul at last heard the prophetic words he had been waiting for! *"Separate me Barnabas and Saul* (Paul) *for the work whereunto I have called them"* (Acts 13:2).

The Holy Spirit said, *". . . for the work whereunto I have called them."* Paul knew he was predestined for this! He could remember the prophecies which were spoken over him when he was first saved, prophecies which said, *"He is a chosen vessel unto me, to bear my name before the Gentiles and kings, and the children of Israel"* (Acts 9:15).

From the very outset of his life in Christ, Paul knew he had an important destiny. He knew he would play a major role in the kingdom of God. But it took thirteen years of preparation before those prophetic words would begin to come to pass in his life. During that time, his character and moral flaws, his pride, and his attitudinal faults were exposed, dealt with by God, and confronted by the men whom God placed over him.

(For more on the subject of how God calls and prepares us for ministry, I highly recommend Bob Yandian's book, *Calling and Separation*, also published by Pillar Books.)

At the end of those thirteen years, Paul said, "*We were allowed of God to be put in trust. . .*" (First Thessalonians 2:4).

The phrase "to be put in trust" is an old Greek phrase which means "to be put in public office, such as a mayor or governor." By using this phrase, Paul is telling us, "It took a long time, but after a series of hard trials and tests through the years, God finally deemed me fit to be used by Him in a public capacity." In other words, he passed his leadership test, and God saw him fit to be trusted in ministry.

But that wasn't the end of the tests and trials for Paul's life! Paul concludes this verse by saying, "*not as pleasing men, but God, which trieth our hearts.*" Because this is present tense in the Greek language, he is telling us, "After all the trials and tests I've been through in my past, God is *still* trying my heart today, making sure I *remain* fit for public service."

This means our leadership fitness is always being monitored and reviewed by God. He is watching to see how we respond to situations, how we are walking in love toward people, how serious we are about the positions He has assigned to us, and how we handle His Word. "After passing all of those earlier tests," Paul says, "the tests aren't over yet! God is still trying our hearts."

Do not be discouraged if it takes time for your dream to become a reality in your life! God never gets in a hurry, because godly character is more important to Him than gifts, talents, or temporary successes in the eyes of our comtemporaries.

You need time to prepare, change, and grow right now, so that when you are finally promoted into a visible position of leadership, you'll have what you need internally and spiritually to keep you in that place, established with the right heart attitude.

Your Ultimate Guarantee for a Victorious Future

According to Peter, there is a way to guarantee yourself that when your leadership comes, it will be fruitful and lasting. He said, *"Giving all diligence, add to your faith virtue; and to virtue knowledge; and to knowledge temperance; and to temperance patience; and to patience godliness; and to godliness brotherly kindness; and to brotherly kindness charity"* (Second Peter 1:5-7).

Then, in verse 8, we are given this glorious promise: *"For if these things be in you, and abound, they make you that ye shall neither be barren nor unfruitful in the knowledge of our Lord Jesus Christ."*

What a promise! If these things be in you and abound, you'll never be barren or unfruitful in your life! But here's the clincher! It takes time to develop all of these things in your life. That's why Peter begins with, *Giving all diligence.* It takes great diligence and tremendous commitment to develop these wonderful attributes in your life.

Here's another reason to be encouraged about where you are in life right now: You need to make wise use of this time by sending your roots down deep into the character of Christ by developing faith, virtue, temperance, patience, godliness, brotherly kindness, and charity. It should be obvious to you that you can't develop all of these overnight. You've got to give diligence and take time to make these things a reality in your life.

In Joshua, chapter one, God had chosen to call Joshua into a position of prominence, but years had gone into this selection. God had been watching for faithfulness, courage, character, moral values, and right responses to varying and difficult situations. He had been looking for someone with enough character to carry the kind of anointing that Israel's leader would need. He had been looking to see who was really committed enough to step into the position of leadership and maintain that position without becoming morally shipwrecked.

During the years of waiting, God was giving Joshua time to send his roots down deep. Then, when it was time for him to lead, he would be strong enough to weather any storm that came against him, just like the tree described in Psalm One.

What Happened to the Other Ten Spies?

I've often wondered what happened to the other spies who went to check out the Promised Land with Joshua and Caleb, but came back with a far different report. What did they do with their lives? What did they accomplish? How did they die?

All of them had the same potential Joshua had. If they hadn't, Moses wouldn't have sent them out and trusted them with a dangerous mission. They were Joshua's comtemporaries, his fellows, his associates, and his peers. What happened to them?

While they had the potential to become great leaders, because they limited their faith and thinking, they were eliminated from God's plan. Rather than move into the Land of Promise, they died in the wilderness, unknown, old has-been's of a previous generation, probably very regretful they had not made wiser choices when they were younger.

People like this, who miss their opportunities in life, usually become critical and bitter about others. Rather than rejoice when other leaders succeed, they nit-pick everything the successful leader does, saying, "I think it should be done this way," or, "I think it should be done that way." Or, "If I was the leader, I'd do it like this."

The truth of the matter is, they are not the leader, and they should keep their negative thinking to themselves. It is their fault they are where they are today, and if they want their *situation* to change then *they* must change. Other people are not their problem. *They* are their problem, and there is nothing more grievous than seeing someone who once had great opportunity and potential become old, hard-hearted, bitter, and cynical. What a waste of life!

Joshua's attitude made the difference in his life. He was willing to go the extra mile, lay down his life, and serve for years without recognition under the leadership of Moses. As a result, when all the other spies were left behind to die as old men in the wilderness, he was still pliable in the hands of God and was still being used in a powerful way.

Cynical people are usually people who once had great promise, but, because of wrong decisions based on pride or unbelief, have been left along the way. Only those who have been diligent and faithful to submit to authority in every position God has placed them have gone forward in the adventure of life.

Those with a right spirit like Joshua's submit to God in all areas of their life while in their present circumstances, no matter how difficult, challenging, impossible, tedious, or frustrating.

When Your New Assignment Seems Impossible

God continued to tell Joshua, *"Moses my servant is dead: now therefore arise, go over this Jordan. . ."*

Joshua's ministry was beginning on the heels of Moses' death, and his first assignment had been given: lead all of these people over the Jordan River into the Land of Promise.

At that particular time, the waters were flowing out of the river's banks and the currents were dangerously wild. People were probably wondering if Joshua had any leadership ability, because he was so new. Then, when he tells them they are going to cross the river at flood stage, they most likely thought their doubts about him were right!

I can almost hear them saying, "Lead us across the Jordan at this time? Don't you realize the river is at flood stage right now? Where is your mind? Do you intend to tell us that God actually told you to lead us over that river at this exact time? What kind of God would tell you to do such a crazy thing? This isn't even logical, Joshua!" Yet, it wasn't any crazier than Moses parting the Red Sea and the children of Israel walking through on dry ground!

That, however, was Moses, and this was Joshua — who, in their minds, surely could never be the kind of leader that Moses was! There was only one Moses, right? *That is precisely the reason that God initiated Joshua's ministry with a supernatural challenge.*

Something had to happen which would immediately prove to the Israelites that Joshua really was God's man, and a miracle similar to the parting of the Red Sea would be just strong enough to make the point.

Place yourself in Joshua's shoes. How do you think he felt when he heard the Holy Spirit tell him, "Cross over the Jordan River!" He knew the river was at flood stage, and he would probably take a lot of criticism from some of the people for suggesting such a ridiculous idea. What a big step of faith this would be for the outset of his ministry!

He probably would have preferred a simpler command to start out with. Something like, "Teach people to pray," or "Believe me to heal all of your sick." Instead, God laid before Joshua an awesome task: lead millions of people across a river when they don't want to cross it and at the worst time of year!

75

Sometimes, when God finally separates a man or woman to do a difficult task, He does not give them the leisure of taking tiny, baby steps in the beginning. Because their new assignment is so important, He may require them to do something monumental right at the start, to show the followers that their new leader has what it takes, and to prove to the new leader that the Holy Spirit is with them.

As the Jordan River parted and the Israelites had passed through on dry ground, no one — including Joshua — questioned Joshua's anointing again. That supernatural intervention of God validated his ministry in the eyes of the whole nation.

There is a negativism in human nature, a result of sin, that causes people to sit back, watch, and wonder when people will fail. They may verbally express support, but quietly and inwardly there may be unspoken reservations about someone who takes a step of faith.

People sit, wait, and watch. If your step of faith fails, or if you do not follow through on your commitment, you will build an assurance in them that you really can't hear the voice of God or that your vision was bigger than your faith.

If, however, they see you actually do what you said you would do — something stupendous that bears great fruit — you will have won their hearts over. The next time you announce you are going to do something outrageous and wild, they will believe you!

This was important in Joshua's ministry, because he was going to lead the people of God to do many naturally outrageous things. He would lead them into battles where they were outnumbered. Many times, according to the facts of the situation, they should have been slaughtered, but they were not.

The parting of the Jordan River not only established the people's confidence in Joshua's leadership, but it also built Joshua's confidence. When those waters parted, I'm sure a new surge of supernatural faith rose up in Joshua's heart as he really realized, "It's true! God really is with me! The same kind of anointing that was on Moses is now on me! I can see it!"

Later, he would command the sun to stand still, and it would remain still for another day. Who would ever think such a thing would be possible? But after the parting of the Jordan River, why not speak to the sun, too? Command it to obey so that the plan of God could be fulfilled.

Don't be afraid to accept the new assignment which God has given to you! It may look large, awesome, and out-rageous to your natural mind, but if God has called you, He has also anointed you for that situation.

When the waters part before you and you pass through your predicament unharmed, there will be a wonderful new confidence in you, a knowing and assurance that you really are right smack in the middle of God's will for your life. And there is no greater confidence than knowing you really are in the right place at the right time in God's plan!

Don't Sit on the Banks

The worst thing you could ever do would be to sit on the banks of that river and wonder, "Would it really part if I take this step of faith?"

That's what most people do!

They sit, they watch, and they think and think about whether or not they should step out in faith and obey. They watch other people take the big leap, and they even read biographies of other men and women who have achieved greatness because they acted on a word from God to do the impossible. But for themselves, they sit and think until, finally, they end up doing absolutely nothing — and then they wonder where all the excitement and adventure is in their lives!

I'll tell you where the adventure is — across the river! The adventure begins when you start moving, focused on the future! When you put your foot into the brink of the waters, you'll experience a surge of faith and excitement like you've never known before in your life. And when those waters part for you, you'll know a dimension of faith that only the brave and daring can come to know.

Years ago, I knew a young man with great potential, but his greatest hindrance to releasing that potential was fear and insecurity. He was a thinker, a planner, and an organizer. All of that was good and necessary, but he allowed those gifts to interfere with the command of God to take a step of faith. They became a stronghold against the will of God.

Opportunity after opportunity presented itself to this man. I watched as he sat on the banks, thinking, thinking, thinking. He would think so long about whether or not to accept a new opportunity that the opportunity would pass right by him. Time after time I watched him do this.

Finally, I said to him, "Recognize what God is doing when He is opening a door for you. You've got to see that God is giving you a green light and obey what the Holy Spirit is telling you. Quit allowing your mind and your fears to keep you from stepping out from where you are to where God wants you to be."

Sadly, today he is still sitting on the banks, looking into the dangerously wild river, wondering what would happen if he would step out in faith to accept a new calling, a new assignment, a new opportunity in life. The chains that bind him are not made of iron, but they are just as real. He has placed these chains on himself, and the longer he sits and stares, thinking and wondering but never acting, the stronger the chains become.

If you've been preparing for this moment, if your pastor or your spouse acknowledges this is God's time for you to enter a new phase of His plan for your life, then step out into those waters and watch what God Almighty will do for you! When those waters begin to part, you will have entered a new realm of living from which there is no return. You'll never *want* to go back to where you once were.

You'll have the faith, courage, and perseverance to step into the next river and into the next, the next and the next. With each experience, the faithfulness of God will build a foundation of confidence in your heart to face your next challenge more boldly and confidently.

Don't allow fear to stop you dead in your tracks. Don't get bogged down and lose the vision which God gave to you. It is time for you to push all those things aside and start focusing on your future.

What is God telling you to do?

Are you absolutely sure that it is the voice of God you are hearing?

If you are sure it is what you're supposed to do, then pick your feet up and step forward into your future. The waters in front of you may look dangerously wild, but rather than focus on all the problems and impossibilities staring at you, make the choice to look forward with faith and start focusing on your future.

Yes, you must be realistic about your own talents, gifts, and finances. You must be realistic about the problems you are facing. If they are a result of your own actions or lack of actions to correct them, then you need to set those things right before you step out to take another big leap of faith.

If, however, your personal life is in order and you've been sending your roots down deep into Christ and His Word, if you've been serving, preparing, and training for this moment and, now you know that your time has come, welcome to your point of no return!

Challenge, conquest, and victory lay before you! The realm of life you are about to enter is more satisfying than anything money could ever buy and more gratifying than any temporal feelings of security could ever afford you.

There is nothing to compare with knowing that you are right in the middle of God's will for your life!

God Wants to Give You Something Wonderful!

God continued to speak to Joshua, *"Moses my servant is dead: now therefore arise, go over this Jordan, thou, and all this people, unto the land which I do give to them, even to the children of Israel."*

I want you to especially notice that God said *"unto the land which I do give to them. . ."* The Land of Promise was just beyond the Jordan River. They were nearly there already! They had heard about it, they had prayed for it, and they had believed to enter the Land of Promise for many years.

On their journey to the place God had prepared for them, they had to deal with rebellions, famines, scorching heat of the desert, poisonous snakes that killed many of them, forty years of wandering back and forth on the same trails. Lastly, the beloved leader who was to take them to the Promised Land died before they ever got there. What a journey that had been!

Through all the trials and temptations they faced, however, many of them, like Joshua, had kept the vision God had given them for a better place and a better life. They had a better dream, and dreams have power. They sustain the fire for the vision, which we need in order to keep going when times become difficult.

Though the older generation who had fled Egypt had been prohibited from entering the Promised Land, the vision of that land flowing with milk and honey had been imparted to their children. The older people remembered the provision of Egypt, which is why they kept looking back again and again. But the younger generation had been born in the desert, grown up in the desert, and had never known life outside of that dusty, barren place.

The idea of a clean, beautiful, green land that flowed with milk and honey must have been an incredible dream for these children! Now they stood on the banks of the Jordan and they could look across and see the land they had dreamed about their entire lives. There it was!

That's when God told Joshua, "*. . . arise, go over this Jordan, thou, and all this people, unto the land which I do give to them, even to the children of Israel.*" Imagine how exciting that prophetic word must have been to those who had been waiting their whole lives for this moment! The dream was happening! The vision their parents had imparted to them was unfolding right in front of them!

Then God dropped the bombshell that brought them back to reality. He continued to say, "*Every place that the sole of your foot shall tread upon, that have I given unto you, as I said unto Moses*" (Joshua 1:3).

You and God are Partners in Fulfilling Your Future

The only thing that is totally free in this world is God's grace. Grace for salvation, grace for the infilling of the Holy Spirit, grace for deliverance, grace to empower you to witness, grace to sanctify you, grace to heal you — all of these come to you directly as a result of God's marvelous, wonderful grace!

But if you are going to be saved, YOU must pray. If you desire to be delivered, YOU must desire to be delivered. If you wish to become a witness, YOU must open your mouth and speak. If you want the Holy Spirit to sanctify you, YOU must have the desire to live a pure and holy life. If God is going to heal you, YOU must use your faith to receive it. God gives all of these wonderful things freely, but our actions, our attitudes, and our faith are directly involved in receiving them.

Likewise, if you are going to see the vision God gave you come to pass in your life, YOU are going to have to get involved in making it happen. God will provide the grace you need to achieve it, but YOU must be God's partner in accomplishing your vision.

God told the Israelites, "I'm giving you the land!" That is, "I'm giving you every place that you put the sole of your foot upon!" This was not an unconditional, unlimited promise. God was saying, "It's yours *if* you do your part! I'll give it to you, *but* you've got to take it!"

In other words, God was telling them, "As long as you sit on this side of the Jordan and simply look at the Land of Promise and ponder it, it's not yours and never will be! If, however, you pass over the river and put your foot on the land, I'll give that particular piece of land to you. As you move ahead and place your feet on additional land, I'll give that to you, too. Every place that the soles of your feet touch is the territory that will become yours!"

When the Lord told us to begin a traveling teaching ministry, Denise and I did something that may sound rather foolish. However, at the time we were completely inspired by the promise that every place our feet tread upon would be given to us.

We had been praying and asking the Holy Spirit to show us how to get more meetings. This was when we only had five scheduled for the next two months. So we took our great big map of the United States off the wall and laid it on the floor. Then we began to walk across the states God was speaking to us about, proclaiming that every place we stepped was ours!

This may have looked crazy to others, but to us it was serious business! And do you know, God honored our craziness! As we traveled around the country for those first five meetings, we repeated our proclamation of faith, and it wasn't long before we were receiving all kinds of calls from the states we first walked upon on our map and then visited in our travels.

God does everything in steps, and *we* have to take them! In order for Joshua and the people of Israel to receive God's promise, they had to get up and do some walking! Sitting on the banks, lazily thinking and wondering what to do, and fretting over the future was not going to bring them closer to the place God wanted them to be.

They already knew the will of God. Now it was time for them to do something!

Chapter Five
Five Primary Reasons People Fail in Life

There are many reasons people stay on the banks of the river, never to venture out into a walk of obedience, faith, and power. In my previous book, *Dream Thieves*, I discussed hindrances which come against your dream from outside sources. I also touched briefly on one that was far more personal — you! It is this area that I want to discuss in more detail in this chapter.

In my own experience, and as I observe and talk to other believers, I have found five primary vices that will hinder you from getting up and doing something valuable in this life. There are actually many more than these, but the five I will discuss are basic to every human being, and they are all very closely related to each other. When one is present, you are sure to find some, if not all, of the others.

Just one of these carnal roadblocks can keep you from moving forward into the future God has designed for you. Thus, it is imperative that you rid yourself of them through the sanctifying power of the Holy Spirit. Their existence in your life will make it very difficult, if not impossible, for you to fulfill the assignment God wishes to give you.

The five primary hindrances you must especially be aware of are *laziness, unrealistic fantasies, slothfulness, creature comforts, and believing a bad report*. Every believer must deal with all of these things to one degree or another, so don't get under condemnation if you are described in the next few pages! Rather, let the Holy Spirit give you His plan for getting free and staying free from them, and then be diligent to stick with His plan. Any of these five vices have the power to knock you out of the game!

Reason Number One: Laziness

The Bible has a lot to say about lazy people, and none of it is good! According to Scripture, the lazy person is a "sluggard" (which means just what it sounds like!) who has nothing but poverty in his future.

How do you know if you are being lazy?

Lazy people usually lie around and waste a lot of time doing nothing. Basically, instead of acting on God's Word and obeying the Holy Spirit, they choose to do what they feel like doing when they feel like doing it.

Simply put, laziness is a very subtle form of rebellion.

You can recognize a lazy person if they are usually idle, sluggish, and lethargic. They sleep long hours and take naps whenever possible. They are prone to simply sit and vegetate, then complain about how hard and difficult their way of life is for them.

This state of laziness has a tranquilizing effect on your body and mind. If you don't deal with it, if you don't get up and begin doing something with purpose, it will eventually put you into a state of complete deception. You will begin procrastinating about everything you need to do and waste your life by spending time selfishly and foolishly.

Listen to what the Bible says about sluggards:

"How long wilt thou sleep, O sluggard? When wilt thou arise out of thy sleep? Yet a little sleep, a little slumber, a little folding of the hands to sleep: So shall thy poverty come as one that travelleth, and thy want as an armed man" (Proverbs 6:9-11).

"The sluggard will not plow by reason of the cold; therefore shall he beg in harvest, and have nothing" (Proverbs 20:4).

These verses describe the sluggard as someone who basically sits around and does nothing. Rather than work and prepare for the future, they sit and sleep. Although they may have dreams, desires, and ambitions, they are too lazy and thus have no energy to pursue any of them.

The Word of God declares that this kind of person has no future. By refusing to invest time, energy, and hard work into the future right now, when the harvest begins to finally come in for others, the sluggard will not be a partaker of those same blessings. By doing nothing to accomplish something with their lives, they prevent themselves from achieving anything of value in life.

Lazy people often complain about having no energy. Of course they have no energy! All you have to do is talk to a bedfast person at a nursing home to find out that when all you do is lie around, you lose your energy. After doing nothing for months on end, just a walk down the hall is a major effort!

If you sit and do nothing for weeks or months but watch television programs or sleep away the time, you will lose energy and have a hard time getting back into the flow of things afterward. Your behavior has put your body into a state of sedation. To get it back on course, you have to decide to get up and move, regardless of whether or not you feel like it.

Laziness is a choice.

Let me ask you, how many of the lazy people you know are also successful? None! The Bible instructs the lazy person to look to the ant in Proverbs 6:6. Why the ant? Because the ant is constantly working, building, digging, tunneling, and preparing — and then starts the whole process all over again without ever taking a minute's break!

No creature in the whole world is more industrious and self-motivated than the ant. Go look at an ant hole or an ant farm. It is remarkable to see them moving so fast, so diligently, so consistently, as if the future of the whole world depended upon them and their actions.

The Book of Proverbs teaches that this is the way we should order our lives. Yes, we should take a vacation now and then. Yes, we should not overwork our bodies and push ourselves beyond what is healthy. But don't worry about it, because you probably haven't done that much work yet!

The human body can do much more than we think it can! We barely use one tenth of our mind's capacity, and most of us eat and sleep much more than necessary. If you look at people who have really made an impact in this world, they work hard, they push themselves, and they are constantly trying to develop their minds and become more creative in the way they do things.

You can do much more than your flesh will ever tell you! Your flesh will always say, "Slow down, don't do anymore, you've already done too much. Give yourself a break! You deserve to sit and do nothing."

If you're so tired that you can't even move, then you need to sit down and take a rest. However, don't allow your flesh to deceive you by telling you you've already done more than any "average" person would do and you deserve a break. You were never called by God to be "average!"

Turn off the television and get up and clean the kitchen! Mow the yard! Pull out the calculator, get your checkbook, and start correcting all the financial problems you've created by ignoring things too long! Quit talking about how tired you are, and go contribute something to life!

Many lazy people also eat all the time, because food has become their primary source of companionship and entertainment. If you fall into this category, don't get mad at me! You know it's true!

If you are lazy and overweight, you don't eat because you are hungry, you eat because you are bored! To make matters worse, you usually eat the kinds of foods that make you feel more tired. Potato chips, cookies, fried foods, sugar products, soft-drinks, excessive amounts of meat and fat — all of these can actually begin to put you to sleep!

Years ago, I suffered a terrible bout of depression. I prayed and tried everything I knew to change this horrible dread that was consuming my life. I had everything to live for, yet I was so depressed that I didn't want to go on living.

I'll never forget how grateful I was when a visiting speaker came to our church and, just in passing, mentioned the depression-like effects of sugar on people who consume too much. I felt I had been set free when this man finished talking! I turned to my wife and said, "Sweetheart, I think it's sugar! I think that's what's wrong with me!"

I went home that day and cut nearly all sugar out of my diet. Within one week that awful, dreadful depression that had gripped me for so long was completely gone! Since then, I've never had another bout of depression like it.

It may not sound deeply spiritual to talk about what we eat, but the fact of the matter is, if people would change what they eat, they would have more energy. In most cases, depression is not demonic, it is dietetic. If you don't believe me, change your diet and see what happens to your general outlook on life!

Even if you are not dealing with depression or laziness, you still need to watch what you eat. It is a waste of life to spend hour upon hour eating. If you are lonely, get involved in some area of ministry at your church and make some friends. If you need to be entertained, do something productive with your time! Read a book, devote more time to developing your business, or see what you can do to help somebody else.

Your life is too precious to be thrown away by doing nothing. Furthermore, your mind is too sacred to let the world of television fill it with trash and unbelief. Watching too much television goes hand in hand with overeating.

What are you accomplishing by watching television all the time? Be realistic! All you have done is use a great deal of your precious time to pour worldly thoughts, pictures, and philosophies into your soul. Now it's going to take some time and commitment to unprogram all the garbage you've allowed ungodly, carnal people to put into your mental computer.

Turn the television off and pick up the Word of God to be renewed in the spirit of your mind (Ephesians 4:23). It's time for you to *put off the old man with his deeds and put on the new man which is renewed in knowledge after the image of him that created him* (Colossians 3:9-10).

Make a commitment to the Lord and to yourself that you are going to develop the gifts, talents, abilities, and the callings of God upon your life. Defeat laziness, bad eating habits, and television addiction by getting your mind so renewed that when God says, "It's time for you to step out into the plan that I have for your life," you won't think twice about it!

Reason Number Two:
Unrealistic Fantasies

If you are lazy, watch too much television, and eat incorrectly, most likely you will also be subject to unrealistic fantasies. Because you are not following God's plan for your life, enjoying real-life experiences and relationships, or living a healthy life, your perception of reality will become distorted. Your imagination will run wild in all the wrong directions!

Rather than working hard and giving it all you've got to see your dreams manifest, you sit and fantasize about accomplishments and experiences which are completely impractical and will never occur. You wait for that golden moment when you'll finally get your break in life, without moving a muscle to do your part, and assuming God will just simply drop your dream right in your lap one day!

Read what Proverbs 28:19 says about people who live in an unreal world of fantasy, *"He that works his ground will have abundant food, but he that chases after fantasies will have his fill of poverty"* (NIV).

This is one of my favorite verses! As a matter of fact, it has been one of the guiding scriptures of my life. According to this verse, if you want to eat, which means, if you want to experience prosperity and blessing in your life, then get up and begin plowing your ground!

Harvests don't happen accidentally! You have to break up that hard, fallow ground you are standing on right now, turn and prepare the soil, and then plant some seeds. And that's not all! Once the soil is prepared and the seeds are planted, they have to be watered and watched over.

You've got to walk through your garden and search for the smallest hint of insects, pests, and weeds. You've got to get down on your hands and knees and pull the weeds out one by one. After days and days of careful watching and hard work, your precious seeds will begin to grow and pierce the top-soil, reaching upward to the sun.

When the plants have reached maturity and it's time for harvest, then you've got to go into the field to pick the harvest when it is ripe. If you let the crops sit too long, the bugs will get them. Timing is everything when it comes to harvest.

That's the way it is with your life, too. If you are going to reap a blessing in your life, it will be because you got involved with the Holy Spirit in making it happen. You must view your life as though it is a huge garden. Although God miraculously causes you to grow, you must do your part by weeding and working wherever He directs.

The most important thing you can do when you get a word from God is to work your ground. You may not think this sounds very spiritual at first, but you will bear fruit. Jesus said in John 15:8, *"Herein is my Father glorified, that ye bear much fruit; so shall ye be my disciples."*

It is not fun to buckle down and work your ground. You don't see stars every time you go out to plant seed in the field. Every time you pull out the hose and turn on the water you get wet and muddy, and it is not something that you want to tell everybody about! "Come over and watch me water the garden and dig in the mud!" But in order for your life to bear fruit, it will require phenomenal amounts of hard work and effort. You've got to have a vision for what God wants your life to be, and then you've got to go after it with all of your spirit, mind, and body.

This is having a realistic outlook on life!

Remember, the Bible says you reap what you sow (Galatians 6:7). If you only fantasize about your future, never actually putting your hand to the plow and putting a little elbow grease into the project, you will only reap more fantasy, and your future will be jammed with poverty and the lack of God's blessings.

People who successfully move into the next God-ordained phase of their lives put all of their strength and energy into seeing their dreams become a reality. With the power of the Holy Spirit working inside and alongside of them, they are a certain winner!

Furthermore, there is a significant difference between a fantasy and a dream. Dreams are born by the Spirit of God and cause you to reach up for all you can possibly be in Jesus Christ. A real word from the Lord will motivate you and give you the strength to crucify your flesh, say "no" to fear, and be conformed to His image.

Fantasies won't do any of that! Fantasies are merely temporary, fleeting pauses from reality. They hinder us from doing anything valuable and practical in this life by their narcotic effect on our minds. They may temporarily make us feel euphoric, but when we wake up to reality and the effect wears off, we see that the kitchen is still dirty, the bills are still unpaid, the marriage is still in trouble, the kids still need to be bathed, and the yard still needs to be mowed.

People who passively wait for success can kiss their dreams farewell. The joy and fulfillment they've fantasized about will go to the man or woman who is practical enough to start working their ground right now.

Those believers who unrealistically expect the victories of life to come to them, do not understand life! Victory, joy, and fulfillment do not float on a cloud that suddenly and unexpectedly drops down into our lives. Success is obtained through desire and hard work, which is why it tastes so sweet when it finally comes!

It's easier to fantasize because it only involves your imagination. But for you to truly find fulfillment, you must hear from God, receive His plan and dream for your life, and then go out and do it. Only His will can keep you planted in reality!

Furthermore, where a fantasy gives you the illusion of perfection with no effort, your word from God will demand that you grow up, change, and allow the Holy Spirit to work in your heart and mind. By working your ground instead of living in a fantasy, you will gain more than a harvest. You will be changed into the person God has created you to be!

Reason Number Three: Slothfulness

Slothfulness is such a deceptive, subtle, and totally destructive enemy of the believer. Because of this, I spent the better part of chapter three of *Dream Thieves* discussing it. Where laziness is a discipline problem, slothfulness is an attitude problem, and they are very closely related.

The lazy person rebels against God's will for their lives by choosing to do nothing; the slothful person chooses to do God's will outwardly, but inwardly retains a neutral and lukewarm attitude toward the things of God. They go through the motions and for the most part will say and do all the right things, but inside their fire and passion for God and serving Him has nearly gone out.

"The way of the slothful man is as an hedge of thorns" (Proverbs 15:19).

"Slothfulness casteth into a deep sleep; and an idle soul should shall suffer hunger" (Proverbs 19:15).

These scriptures make it abundantly clear that the slothful person has no future. Their own lack of drive and passion to please God will cause their life to be overgrown with weeds that should have been dealt with much earlier in life. However, because they were slothful, they shut their eyes to these problems and let them continue in their life unchecked. Now the problems have become so bad, so over-grown, that their way has become a hedge of thorns.

"He also that is slothful in his work is brother to him that is a great waster" (Proverbs 18:9).

How would you like for your work to be known as a waste? Let me ask you, what do other people say about you and your work? Are you known by your peers as a very industrious, enthusiastic worker, or do people think of you as a silent partner or a fifth wheel?

What does God think of your attitude? If you were to stand in front of the judgment seat of Christ today, would you be satisfied with the manner in which you have carried out God's plan for your life, or would you be embarrassed, knowing you only half-heartedly and begrudgingly did what God asked you to do?

The Apostle Paul was so aware that he would give account for what he had done as a Christian, he said, *"Wherefore we labour, that, whether present or absent, we may be accepted of him. For we must all appear before the judgment seat of Christ; that everyone may receive the things done in his body, according to that he hath done, whether it be good or bad"* (Second Corinthians 5:9-10).

The judgment seat of Christ is rarely taught in Christian circles today, which is too bad. Our attitude changes dramatically if we are constantly aware that one day we will stand before the Lord eyeball to eyeball and give account for how responsibly or irresponsibly we lived, for our attitude toward Him and toward His calling on our lives. There will be no fast talking or excuses on that day!

Slothful people always seem to be making excuses for themselves, naming reasons why they didn't do what they promised, or why they have failed along the way. Rather than honestly saying, "I just didn't do what was required," they attempt to hide their lukewarm, "I-don't-really-care" attitude in the disguise of excuses.

Solomon made mention of what the excuse-making slothful people do in Proverbs 22:13, where the slothful man says, *"There is a lion without, I shall be slain in the streets."* That's the equivalent of saying, "Sometimes there are earthquakes in our state, so I'm going to stay home in case an earthquake happens today."

Talk about stupidity! If we are going to sit around and talk about "what if's," we'll never do anything in life! That, however, is just how absolutely ridiculous and absurd the excuses of the slothful can be! Rather than take on the responsibility and own up to the fact that deep inside they are not real keen on serving the Lord, they blame everyone and everything else for their failures and frustrations.

The lists of excuses people make for not doing what they should do would take another entire book. (That might be a fun book to write and read — the excuses of the slothful are outrageously ridiculous!)

Even the Lord Jesus Christ spoke about excuse makers. In the Lord's mind, excuse making is so serious that He said those who make excuses for themselves would eventually be eliminated from blessing and further participation in the plan of God. He flatly said that they would be replaced with someone else who is more willing.

In Luke 14:16-24, the Lord Jesus says, *"A certain man made a great supper, and bade many: and sent his servant at supper time to say to them that were bidden, Come; for all things are now ready.*

"And they all with one comment began to make excuse. The first said unto him, I have bought a piece of ground, and I must needs go and see it: I pray thee have me excused.

"And another said, I have bought five yoke of oxen, and I go to prove them: I pray thee have me excused.

"And another said, I have married a wife, and therefore I cannot come.

"So that servant came, and shewed his lord these things. Then the master of the house being angry said to his servant, Go out quickly into the streets and lanes of the city, and bring in hither the poor, and the maimed, and the halt, and the blind.

"And the servant said, Lord, it is done as thou has commanded and yet there is room.

"And the Lord said unto the servant, Go out into the highways and hedges, and compel them to come in, that my house may be filled.

"For I say unto you, That none of those men which were bidden shall taste of my supper."

On my own staff, one thing I absolutely cannot tolerate is excuses. If someone has forgotten to do something they were supposed to do, then it is better to just say you forgot. Don't make up some ridiculous story that doesn't hold an ounce of water! Just say you forgot! That is human and it is forgivable, but please don't make up an excuse!

Occasionally, we have conflicts that keep us from doing something we have promised to do. But don't invent a crazy spiritual reason for why you can't do it. Just say, "I have other plans. May I be released from this responsibility right now?" If you don't want to do something you've been given to do, then ask, "Can someone else do this?"

If you failed to follow through on an assignment that was strategic to a major operation because you just didn't think it was *that* important, rather than lay out a whole detailed story about why you didn't follow through, just apologize and admit your failure.

Straightforward honesty is the way slothfulness can be defeated. You must be honest with yourself and with God about your inner feelings and attitudes. If you continue to make excuses, you are deceiving yourself and lying to God. According to Luke 14:16-24, even Jesus is disgusted with people who make excuses.

If you have failed in this area of your life, don't get depressed, just do something about it. Recognize that excuse-making is sin and you must stop doing it. Confess your sin in this area of your life according to First John 1:9, and God will forgive you and cleanse you of this subtle unrighteousness.

Closely related to making excuses is blaming someone else. Most of the slothful people I have known blame their difficulties on the devil or someone else. That way, they do not have to be responsible for their own lives. Everything is someone else's fault!

Even if a person has been under some kind of devilish attack, that is still no excuse for failure. The Bible clearly teaches that spiritual warfare is an arena where Jesus has given us ultimate authority over every demon and Satan himself. (In my book, *Dressed to Kill*, A Biblical Perspective on Spiritual Warfare and Armor, I give a detailed study on spiritual warfare).

The slothful person is not destroyed by spiritual warfare, but by their own lack of passion for and diligence in pursuing spiritual victory and maturity. The Book of Proverbs tells us that slothful people will be utterly destroyed personally, spiritually, financially, and socially because they were too lazy to get up and attend to the important details in their lives.

In Ecclesiastes 10:18 it says, *"By much slothfulness the building decayeth; and through idleness of the hands the house droppeth through."*

According to this verse, slothfulness can be recognized as a "Who cares?" outlook. This poisonous attitude will ultimately lead to laziness and idleness, and a person who is slothful will be neutralized spiritually, financially, and socially.

If that is you, then it is time for you to stop making excuses, blaming others, and start doing some changing! How do you change? Fellowship with and imitate those who are not slothful! Look to mature believers in your church who have kept their drive, enthusiasm, and love for the things of God consistently over the years. Spend time with them and become their disciple.

Hebrews 6:12 says, *"That ye be not slothful, but followers of them who through faith and patience inherit the promises."* Follow those you see around you who are seeing a harvest of joy and fulfillment through their faith and patience. Imitate their faith and patience.

If you cannot find anyone who fits this description, and there is no one to whom you can turn to help you ignite the fire in your heart for the things of God and keep it burning bright, then follow and imitate Jesus! Romans 13:14 instructs us, *"But put ye on the Lord Jesus Christ, and make not provision for the flesh, to fulfil the lusts thereof."*

It is *your* responsibility to renew your mind with God's Word and pray in the Spirit every day, not only to receive guidance and wisdom, but also to keep your relationship with the Lord thriving and vibrant and a vital part of your daily life. If you do this, you will not fall into slothfulness!

Reason Number Four:
Creature Comforts

Creature comforts are those things which make us comfortable in life, things we think we can't live without, but which are really superficial and unnecessary. They merely make life easier and more convenient. Various examples would be microwave ovens, fast-food restaurants, shopping malls, video stores, and dishwashers.

Now that I live in the former USSR, I have a whole new perspective on the necessity of creature comforts! Once these kinds of things are not available, you realize they aren't so important after all. None of them are vital to our existence, and we rarely miss them anymore.

A nice big house with beautiful carpet, two car garage with two cars in it, new fishing boat parked outside the house, microwave oven, garbage disposal, trash compactor, double-wide refrigerator, jacuzzi bathtub, washer and dryer, sprinkler system in the yard, and a cellular telephone are not absolutely critical to your existence.

It is interesting to me that because young people in the United States have grown up with so many luxuries, they think these are necessities and act like we would be crazy to be without them! One young girl actually asked me, "How do you wash the dishes without a dishwasher?"

"Simple!" I replied. "You fill the sink with hot water and dishwashing detergent and begin washing the dishes by hand." She was horrified that we would have to take an extra ten minutes of our lives to do something so base and old-fashioned!

We have learned what is important and what is not. Water is important, energy to keep your house warm in the winter is important, and food is important. These are not creature comforts, but the absolute necessities of life.

I hope you have a nice big house with a two car garage and with two cars in it. I hope that you have all the nice things I mentioned above. In our day and age, when we're always on the move, having a cellular phone is a great idea. There's nothing wrong with having any of these things — unless their convenience and comfort makes us so snug and warm that we won't leave it all behind to take a step of faith!

That's exactly what happened to the children of Israel. Once they were out in the desert and on their way to the Promised Land, they began to remember Egypt. Life in Egypt was very difficult and sometimes tormenting for the people of God, but after walking around the desert for awhile and seeing nothing but sand and dust, Egypt was looking pretty good!

Their memory began playing tricks on them, and the bondage they experienced under Pharoah was totally overshadowed by thoughts of exotic foods and many other amenities. They moaned and groaned to go back to Egypt so many times, God eventually decreed, "You cannot go into the Land of Promise!"

The truth is, we find out just how serious we really are about fulfilling God's call on our life when we have to give up some things. It is easy to say you would give everything to Jesus when He has never asked you for anything. It is easy to say you would die for Him when you live in a country that has religious freedom.

We find out how committed we are when Jesus Christ finally asks us to step out of our comfort zone into a more challenging walk of faith. What do you say to Him when He tells you to leave behind job security, health insurance, and annual pay increases?

Stepping out of your comfort zone to obey God often requires a deeper crucifixion of the flesh.

In Second Timothy 2:5, the Apostle Paul talks about the attitude we must have to obey God's will for our lives. He says, "*And if a man also strive for masteries, yet he is not crowned, except he strive lawfully.*"

The word strive is from the Greek word *athlesis*, which always describes a man who was involved in tremendous athletic competition. At the time Paul wrote, there were both amateur and professional athletes. If you were an amateur, you were not considered to be a serious contender. If you were a professional, however, it was said you were an athlete who was striving for the mastery.

This kind of athlete was going for the very top, the mastery of his profession. They were determined to be the absolute best. There was not an amateur bone in them; they were totally committed. It is this very word, *athlesis*, describing committed, full-time, professional athletes, which Paul uses in this verse. He asks Timothy and every believer:

"Are you serving the Lord just for fun? Are you an amateur who isn't really committed to go all the way and accept the next assignment God is giving you? Are you serving the Lord because it is popular, convenient, and enjoyable at the moment?

"Or are you a professional, willing to pay any price, undergo any kind of preparation and hardship, bear up under any pressure, and endure it all until you come out the winner?

"Are you really committed?"

We must ask ourselves these questions. It is fun to serve the Lord when it is easy and convenient, but what if God asks you to step out of your life of ease to accept a bigger challenge? That is the moment of discovery, when we find out if we are amateurs or professionals!

If you are sitting on the banks of your life, knowing God is calling you to cross the river and enter a new and greater walk of faith and power, don't look back to Egypt and all its creature comforts! Look across the river into the land of promise! That's where the milk and honey flows!

Keep your eyes on the milk and honey!

That step of faith will eventually reap great, incredible fruit — both materially and spiritually. Whatever you give up to follow God's plan for your life will look pale and insignificant once you have found your place in the Promised Land!

Stepping into the river might mean a little discomfort for a period of time. You may have to deal with currents of opposition you haven't dealt with before. It will definitely require great concentration and wisdom to make it to the other side.

Once you have passed all the temporary discomfort and turbulence that goes with crossing flooded rivers, however, you'll reach the bank of the Promised Land, and the memory of the difficulty of that river will disappear almost instantaneously. One taste of the grapes, milk, and honey, and you'll wonder why in the world it took you so long to get there!

How important are *things* in your life?

Your day of revelation will come when the Lord imparts a new vision to you and, to fulfill that vision, you must take a harder, more challenging route than you are traveling right now, with fewer amenities to enjoy!

Reason Number Five: Believing a Bad Report

Let's return once again to our scenario of sitting on the banks of the Jordan. God has just given you the next phase of your life, which means you must get up and cross that wild, dangerous river. If you look at the raging, foaming currents before you, you'll be so paralyzed with fear that you'll never be able to move again. If you listen to all the doubts and fears the devil and your friends drop in your ear, every ounce of faith you have will drain out of the bottom of your feet and you'll never move a muscle.

The world is full of doom and gloom! There are many multitudes of people who make fortunes reporting bad news. For some crazy reason (I'm sure it is a result of sin) human nature loves to hear and watch bad news!

Have you ever noticed the kind of books they sell on television in the United States? Books like, *The World's Worst Natural Disasters,* or *Learn the Real Story about How Many People Were Killed* in this or that war, or *The Future Economic Downfall of Our Nation and What You Should Do to Prepare!*

Have you ever gone into an airport bookstore to see what kind of books they sell? They sell what they know people will buy! Books like, *The Worst Murders in Texas History, The Tourist Serial Murders, The Nanny Killer, The Chainsaw Massacre Murders,* or *The Nurse from Hell* with the subhead, "How She Gagged, Poisoned and Killed 34

Patients Under Her Watchful Medical Care!" Or, *The Unspoken Dangers of the Airline Industry!*

Negative, negative, negative! What do you think those books will do to your mind? The next time you go to the hospital or need a babysitter, you'll think twice! After reading *The Tourist Serial Murders*, you may never go on another vacation in your life! And by the time you have read that book on the dangers of airplanes, I'm sure you'll really have a good time on your flight that day!

Amazing as it is, this is what people buy! As long as people buy it, others will continue writing it, printing it, and pumping fear out as fast as they can!

What about your newspaper? If a major newspaper in your city decided to report only good news, how many people would read it? If the evening news told only good stories, people would be so bored they would turn it off. Disasters sell newspapers! Horror stories make news ratings go up! Bad news is a multi-billion dollar industry!

When we first moved to the Soviet Union, I was a news freak of the highest magnitude. I didn't know how I was going to live without CNN, the twenty-four-hour cable news network. I was completely addicted to news. When CNN started their news around the world, every thirty minutes, I was in hog-heaven! Now, every thirty minutes, I could hear the same news story over and over again!

I would sit in front of the television whenever I could, waiting and watching for the next bit of information that would be reported. I don't know why I was waiting! You would have thought that the survival of the human race depended upon my hearing the news.

It is my joy to tell you that there is life beyond CNN! For several years, we have had no regular news broadcasts in our lives, and somehow we have survived. There is no ABC, CBS, or NBC for us to watch every night at the regular evening news times. Amazingly enough, our lives continue to flourish!

We didn't even know there was a terrible hurricane that hit Florida or that a riot occurred in Los Angeles until months after they happened. A visitor from the United States mentioned it to us in passing. When the political squabbles were happening in Moscow recently, we missed nearly all of it! We wouldn't have even known about it, but people kept calling from the United States to ask, "Are you all right? Is your family safe?"

The only thing that was upsetting us was all the bad news we were hearing from friends and family in the United States! In the midst of this terrible, potential revolutionary period that we're living in here in the former USSR, we have absolute peace. First, we have peace because of the peace of God that is in us and on us to be here. Second, we have peace because we are not bombarded with bad news all day!

Several months ago, after the presidential elections in the United States and during a time when the new president was introducing many new government policies, I was at our bank in Riga (our capital city) to open an account for our ministry. Suddenly, I noticed they were broadcasting CNN on the television! I asked how they got it, and they told me it was piped into the bank through a special satellite. I was elated ! ! !

Rather than open the bank account, I pulled up a seat and watched ten minutes of the news. By the end of that ten minutes, my stomach was literally churning and felt like it was being tied into knots. Denise sat there with me and was totally shocked when I said, "Forget this! Life is better without all of this information being thrown at us all day!"

In that ten minutes of news, I had heard about the newest reports on the increase of AIDS. I was informed that the auto and airline industries are on the brink of disaster, which could cripple the nation financially. I learned of the push to allow homosexuals in the military, how the nation's education system is failing, that the New York Stock Exchange was going so high that analysts are afraid it will soon crash, and so on.

By the time those ten minutes passed, I felt my spirit and soul had been violated by informational garbage. At that moment, I realized more than ever the impact of bad reports on our minds and spirits. I remembered that the Bible warns us to continually guard our hearts and minds.

When I was a small boy in Sunday school, we used to sing, *"Oh, be careful little eyes what you see. Oh, be careful little eyes what you see. For your Father up above is looking down in love. Oh, be careful little eyes what you see."*

Then we would change the words to, *"Oh, be careful little ears what you hear! Oh, be careful little ears what you hear! For your Father up above is looking down in love. Oh, be careful little ears what you hear!"*

There is a great truth contained in this little song! We need to be careful what we see and careful what we hear! Even more, we need to be careful of who interprets what we see and hear!

The news story about Israel and the PLO signing a peace treaty could be interpreted differently by a whole host of people. An unbelieving news commentator, who has little or no knowledge of the Bible, will give all the positive and negative ramifications of the peace agreement.

A Spirit-filled Bible teacher with a calling to teach end-time events will interpret the news in a totally different way. The unbelieving reporter will just report news and make educated guesses about what could happen. A Bible teacher who understands prophecy, on the other hand, will interpret the news according to the Word of God.

In this particular situation, you can see how the same news story that upsets the peace of news watchers around the nation will fill you with confidence and joy that the Lord is returning soon!

Whoever interprets the news for you is very important. They can encourage you or hinder you in your adventure of faith. Those who influence your thinking have great power over your future.

In Numbers 13, Moses sent his delegation of twelve spies into the Land of Promise to spy out the land. The land was so rich in products that, when the spies came to the brook of Eschol, the clusters of grapes were so big they had to carry them between two spears which were resting on top of the spies' shoulders. The figs and pomegranates were equally as large.

After forty days of searching out the land, the twelve spies returned to Moses to report what they had seen. They said, *"We came unto the land whither thou sentest us, and surely it floweth with milk and honey; and this is the fruit of it"* (Numbers 13:27).

They continued, *"Nevertheless, the people be strong that dwell in that land, and the cities are walled, and very great: and moreover, we saw the children of Anak* (giants) *there"* (verse 28).

Right in the midst of all the negativism, Caleb, one of the twelve spies, spoke up and silenced the people by saying, *"Let us go up at once, and possess it; for we are well able to overcome it"* (verse 30). The other spies saw giants, but Caleb saw fruit.

Though all of these men were on the same mission of espionage, they had radically different interpretations of what they had seen and what the possibilities were in the Promised Land.

As a matter of fact, when Caleb spoke up to encourage the people to believe they could go up and possess the land, one of the other men who went up with him said, *"We be not able to go up against this people; for they are stronger than we"* (verse 31).

God had brought the people to the brink of the river, and it was now time for them to enter into the land they had been promised by the God Who had delivered them from the bondage of Egypt, parted the Red Sea, and provided for them in a miraculous way. But instead of trusting God to take care of them, these ten leaders are afraid He will forsake them if they take one more step of faith.

Verse 32 goes on to tell us, *"And they brought up an evil report of the land which they had searched unto the children of Israel, saying, The land through which we have gone to search it, is a land that eateth up the inhabitants thereof; and all the people that we saw in it are men of great stature. And there we saw the giants, the sons of Anak, which come of the giants; and we were in our own sight as grasshoppers, and so we were in their sight."*

The report of the ten unbelieving spies was evil because it promoted unbelief in the ability of God. When your faith is negated, it is impossible for you to move ahead with your life. Your future, your plans, and your desires are finished the moment you choose to believe it can't be done. That is why this kind of report is called evil by God.

Any report that says you and God are not big enough to do what God has called you to do is evil. If you believe that kind of report, it will annihilate your future.

Through many years of love and patience, God's grace had brought the children of Israel to the edge of their future and now, because they believed the negative report of the ten spies, instead of the positive report of Joshua and Caleb, their future was wiped out.

The whole congregation of Israel wept and cried out when they heard the report of the ten spies. The Bible says they cried all night long, saying, *"Would to God that we had died in the land of Egypt or would to God we had died in this wilderness!"*

God was more than happy to accommodate their prayer request! He forbade them from entering into the Land of Promise! Then, in the midst of the national spiritual crisis, Moses and Aaron, knowing the seriousness of the moment, fell on their faces before God, while Joshua and Caleb declared, *"The land, which we passed through to search it, is an exceeding good land. If the Lord delight in us, then he will bring us into this land, and give it us; a land which floweth with milk and honey. Only rebel not against the Lord, neither fear ye the people of the land; for they are bread for us: their defense is*

departed from them, and the Lord is with us: fear them not"
(Numbers 14:7-9).

The people of Israel were so angry with Joshua and
Caleb for being positive, they threatened to stone them to
death. But immediately, the glory of God appeared in the
tabernacle of the congregation, and God said to them, *"How
long will this people provoke me? and how long will it be ere they
believe me, for all the signs which I have shewed among them . . .
Because all those men which have seen my glory, and my miracles,
which I did in Egypt and in the wilderness, and have tempted me
now these ten times, and have not hearkened to my voice; Surely
they shall not see the land which I sware unto their fathers"*
(Numbers 14:10-11, 22-23).

The people prayed to die in the wilderness and that is
exactly what they got! They should have made a wiser
choice when they heard the two varying reports from the
spies. Had they listened to Joshua and Caleb, they would
have entered into the place that God had prepared for them.
As it was, only their children — led by Joshua and Caleb
forty years later — were allowed to enter into the Land of
Promise, where they experienced victory after victory
against the local inhabitants!

God told Moses why Caleb (and Joshua) would be the
new leadership of Israel. He said, *"Because he had another
spirit with him, and hath followed me fully, him will I bring into
the land whereinto he went; and his seed shall possess it"*
(Numbers 14:24).

Their spirits were different from the other men's. As I
said earlier, the other spies saw giants, but Joshua and Caleb
saw fruit! There was something internally different about
these men that made them focus on victory rather than on
bloodshed, on accomplishment rather than challenge.

Twelve men spied out the land together, but each spy's
interpretation of what they saw was based entirely on their
inner attitude. Those who were filled with faith said, "We
can do it!" Those who were filled with unbelief said, "We'll

die!" Both groups got exactly what they said! Joshua and Caleb went up and possessed the land, and the other ten spies died in the wilderness, just as they had predicted!

Be careful what you see, what you hear, and even more, be careful who interprets the news to you. Make certain the Word of God is your foundation. Had you been there when the ten spies returned from the Land of Promise, whose report would you have believed?

We need to be informed of what is happening so we can pray more intelligently. We need to know what's going on politically so we can voice our opinions and make our will known. That's part of our responsibility as free people. But we do not need to sit around and watch the same news stories of disaster over and over again. We do not need to listen to so many bad reports of what might happen in the future, they paralyze us from moving into the future God has for us!

If God has spoken to you and told you to start a new business, but the evening news reports the nation's economy is bad for new businesses and makes your step of faith look stupid, you need to forget the news and obey God! He knew what the news was going to be before He ever called you to start that business, and He has already devised ways in which you can overcome any obstacle that comes your way.

In closing, I want to mention one possible source of an evil report which is very sensitive to you — your friends and family. I dealt with this in *Dream Thieves*, but again, because it is so important, I wish to reiterate it again.

Your friends and family love you! They don't want you to make a wrong decision or a mistake, to take a turn in your ministry or career that will harm you or set you back. Thank God they love you so much!

You need to listen to them, pay attention to what they say, and then weigh it according to the Word of God and what the Holy Spirit has already spoken to your heart. In the midst of their concerns, they might have some good, godly wisdom you need to hear.

Take all the good counsel you can receive, but draw the line when that counsel turns into fear and unbelief! Respect them and honor them, even thank them for their love, their concern, and their suggestions. The bottom line, however, is that *you* are going to answer for your life, not them.

Usually, our friends and family want to spare us any hardship as we proceed in life. However, for you to do the will of God, you will have to face some hardship along the way. To establish a new business, it will be necessary for you to change your lifestyle for awhile. If you are going to get married, this decision will demand that you learn how to be more sacrificial and accommodate someone else besides yourself.

It's good that our friends and family want to spare us difficulty in life, but let's be realistic! Look at successful and great men and women of God down through history. Like them, if you forge ahead against all the odds, filled with determination, purpose, and Holy Ghost guts, you can do anything God has asked you to do, but you will go through some very difficult and trying times.

Taking the Promised Land was no easy trick! It was true that there were giants in the land and those giants had been eating the inhabitants thereof. Joshua knew, however, that because of God's grace, the defense of the giants was gone and the Lord was with them in their cause.

Thank your precious family and friends for their love and concern. Listen to their counsel in a way that honors them. They truly have some important input which will help you *count the cost*.

Joshua and Caleb knew exactly what they were up against when they said they were well able to take the land. Having been in the land and having explored it thoroughly for forty days, they had seen every blessing and every potential and real danger. They had seen the great clusters of grapes, and they had seen the great walled cities of the sons of Anak. They were not living in a fantasy, nor were they blind or ignorant to the realities of the future.

These men had forty days to think and pray before they stood in front of Israel and said, "We can do it." There was nothing hasty about their faith or their decision.

Hasty decisions usually precipitate hasty failure.

Jesus warned us about acting before thinking! In Luke 14:28-30, he told us, *"For which of you, intending to build a tower, sitteth not down first, and counteth the cost, whether he have sufficient to finish it? Lest haply, after he hath laid the foundation, and is not able to finish it, all that behold it begin to mock him, Saying, This man began to build, and was not able to finish."*

Many projects are easy to start, but it is another thing altogether to finish them! Don't get the cart before the horse and jump too fast on major decisions about your future. Find the will of God and know it inside and out, clear to the bottom of your soul. Count the cost, and make sure you really understand the assignment which you are agreeing to carry out.

That is just common sense!

This is why Proverbs 24:3-4 tells us, *"Any enterprise is built by wise planning, becomes strong through common sense, and profits wonderfully by keeping abreast of the facts"* (TLB).

After the cost is counted and the facts are in, after all your friends and family have given their best advice, after you've taken care what you hear and see and who interprets the news, then arise and cross the river!

Step Forward and Watch the Waters Part!

It was time for Joshua to step into the waters of the Jordan, cross the river, and go back into the land he had spied out years before. The cost was counted, plans had been made, he had been submitted to Moses all those years in preparation for the moment that had now come.

Laziness would have kept him camped on the bank of the Jordan River.

Unrealistic fantasies would have nullified God's plan.

Slothfulness would have brought him to ruin.

The love of creature comforts would have returned him to Egypt.

Believing an evil report would have left him dead in the wilderness.

Make sure that none of these five things are active in your life, or you will have a very difficult time fulfilling God's plan. Once these hindrances have been crucified by the Word of God and the sanctifying power of the Holy Spirit, however, the power of God can operate through you in ways you never dreamed possible!

Pick up your feet and step forward — then watch what happens when the soles of your feet touch those raging, whirling, foaming, turbulent waters of impossibility!

Chapter Six
Understanding Your Boundaries and Perimeters

It is important for us to understand exactly where the Lord wants us to be at this moment in our lives. Whenever we are misplaced in what we are doing, we will experience frustration, heartache, disappointment, failure, and even depression. We'll always be wondering, "Why am I so unhappy and unfulfilled? Why do I always feel like I'm sinking and can hardly keep my head above water?"

Have you ever tried to put a square peg into a round hole? It just doesn't fit! That's exactly what it feels like when you're trying to serve in the wrong place or be someone you were never meant to be! If you are the square peg and either you or someone else has been trying to cram you into that round hole, then you know precisely the kind of frustration I'm talking about!

Knowing Your Calling and Sticking With It

I am gifted by God to teach the Word of God and to write. I love doing these things! I love to study and prepare messages which I know will enable people to live a more victorious life. I love to write, like right now, just knowing God will use the written page to sharpen a believer's understanding and put them on an even surer foundation. That's me! That's what God has called me to do.

For years I thought I had failed as a Christian because I did not have an overwhelming desire to be an evangelist who preached to unbelievers. I even tried to force myself to have a burden for sinners, to make myself enjoy preaching evangelistic messages, to strive to weep for the lost.

When I couldn't drum up these emotions, tons of guilt hounded me! I kept hearing, "What's wrong with you, Renner! Don't you care that people are lost and dying and going to hell?"

I could honestly answer, "Yes, I really do care, but I just don't feel the weight of the world on my heart about this! I'm trying to get a burden!" I would repent for my lack of compassion, even thinking I wasn't really saved. Surely, if I was really saved, I would be shaken to the core over lost people!

I would pray for strength, energy, and vision to see a world that needed tracts, booklets, and personal evangelism if they were ever going to be saved. I attended special training sessions on evangelism which lasted for months. Still, the motivation and drive for being an evangelist never came, which led to more guilt. There were times when I felt like I was a total spiritual failure.

On the other hand, if you talked about teaching the Word of God, my heart would nearly skip a beat for joy! If you discussed teaching new believers all the foundational doctrines of the New Testament, you could hardly keep me in my seat! The maturity of the saints was so exciting to me, I could hardly contain myself when the subject came up!

That's because God has called me to teach the Bible to believers after they have been won through the evangelistic efforts of other people. This does not excuse my personal responsibility to be a witness for Jesus Christ when an opportunity arises. We are all called to be witnesses, and I have personally led many to the Lord.

But we are not all called to have the same identical burdens, visions, and job assignments in the Body of Christ. We all have a different place and part in the plan of God, and every last one of us is vital to fulfilling God's will on this planet.

The Apostle Paul said in First Corinthians 12:12, 15-18, *"For as the body is one, and hath many members, and all the members of that one body, being many, are one body: so also is Christ.*

"If the foot shall say, Because I am not the hand, I am not of the body; is it therefore not of the body?

"And if the ear shall say, Because I am not the eye, I am not of the body; is it therefore not of the body?

"If the whole body were an eye, where were the hearing? If the whole were hearing, where were the smelling?

"But now hath God set the members every one of them in the body, as it hath pleased him."

God predestines our lives by choosing us, convicting us of sin, and drawing us by His Spirit, gloriously saving us, anointing us with His gifts and power, and then placing us in the Body of Christ as it pleases Him.

If He has called you to be a Bible teacher, yet you're trying to be an evangelist, I guarantee you that you will feel like a square peg who is being pushed into a round hole! If He has called you to be an evangelist, yet you are being pressured to teach the Bible, you will also feel miserable!

If you are called to an assistant position and you do it comfortably and with great ease, but others have compelled you to move into an executive leadership role where you are miserable, then go back to doing what you were called and gifted to do!

Many times when people are put into the positions they were never destined to fill, they end up feeling guilty for not liking their job or appreciating their new privileges. Some believers rebuke the devil, thinking he is attacking them in their new prosperity, but still the uneasiness, guilt, and frustration persist. Others pray for more desire and energy to do the job, but never receive it.

If you have accepted an assignment God never intended for you to accept, neither rebuking the devil nor praying for more energy are going to help. If you're in the wrong place, then you do not have a devil problem or a flesh problem. You're just a square peg trying to fit into a round hole! It's as simple as that!

Blessing and contentment will come when you get back into the place God wants you to be. Then, everything will come back into line and your joy will be restored. Your fuzzy perspective will begin to clear up and you'll know you are back on track again.

The challenge is being able to discern your situation! The question is, "Is God trying to call you upward into new, previously unknown territory and, therefore, your flesh is recoiling at the thought, or are you trying to be and do what God never ordained?" Ultimately, only you can answer this question.

Talking with your spouse, your friends, your parents, your pastor, or your employer can be helpful in this case. They may see things more clearly and may be able to help you work through the deception of your own emotions, so you will know what you are really facing. But as I have said before, you are the one who will stand before Jesus Christ and answer for the gifts, callings, and talents in your life.

If you are called to stay home as a wife and mother, then don't bite off more than you can chew by accepting a job with a major corporation. If you're called to work in an administrative role in a large firm, then don't try to launch a professional golfing career. If you are called into full-time ministry, don't go out and start a business.

You need to know exactly where God wants you to be and then get there! If you are already there, don't allow tales of other wonderful careers and positions knock you out of the place God has assigned to your life at this particular time. It might be enjoyable to imagine being somewhere else, far away from all the struggles and realities of your present circumstances, but the hard fact is that this is the place where God has called you to be.

We have already discussed the calamity that comes from living in a fantasy world, and dreaming of "paradise" will only delay the inevitable. Even if you could run off to some desert island, you would find problems there, too! If you could run away to some remote place in the mountains, trouble would visit you sooner or later.

In reality, wherever you go and whatever you do, even in the perfect will of God, you are going to face problems, challenges, and attacks of the enemy. But it's a whole lot easier to walk through the fire and flood when you know you are in God's perfect plan for your life!

Facing the Reality of Taking the Land

As long as you are in this world, and as long as you want to make a difference, you'll have to face life and deal with it straight on. Ignoring it, hiding from it, shutting your eyes and hoping the problems will somehow, some way, disappear is a fantasy of the wildest proportions. This euphoric place you're dreaming about only exists on the pages of fairy tales.

Now don't misunderstand me, there is a great peace, contentment, and joy when you are in God's will. It is a kind of euphoria, but the purpose of the peace of God is to undergird us and carry us through to victory as we face the challenges and hardships He knows we will encounter in serving Him.

The children of Israel dreamed of a land that flowed with milk and honey, and that land was a real, tangible place. But to conquer and possess the land, they had many wild adventures of faith, such as crossing the Jordan River at flood stage (Joshua 3:11-17), taking the city of Jericho (Joshua 6:1-27), battling the inhabitants of Ai (Joshua 7,8), defending their treaty with the Gibeonites by fighting five Amorite kings at one time (Joshua 9,10), and many more.

Their confidence to enter the land was not based on their military might, but rather on the rock solid conviction that they were acting on God's orders. They had received a specific vision, a specific word from God. With that specific word of direction burning in their hearts, they passed over into a land that was full of both conflict and blessing.

They were facing the reality of what it meant to take the land!

Regardless of the enemies they would face, they knew they were in the right place at the right time. The pain they experienced was just normal pain that goes with conquering any new territory. Enemies had to be eliminated, fear destroyed, rebellion put down, strongholds taken, and many miracles wrought.

It is critical that you understand the boundaries and perimeters of your gifts, your callings, and your talents. Knowing your limitations is just as important as knowing all of your potential. As long as you stay within your boundaries, exactly in the place where God has ordained you to be, it doesn't matter how big the devil looks or how great the obstacles appear to be, you have a promise of divine protection and provision!

In that God-called place, you'll have supernatural joy, peace, and contentment, even in the face of giants!

When God called Joshua to lead the people of Israel into the Promised Land, He didn't say, "Take your pick! Choose any piece of land you want! You decide how much land you should have!" Rather, when Joshua led the people into Canaan, he had very specific instructions and a very clear vision of the land that they were to possess.

God told him that every place they set their foot would be theirs, but He went on to specify *where* their feet were to go, *"From the wilderness and this Lebanon even unto the great river, the river Euphrates, all the land of the Hittites, and unto the great sea toward the going down of the sun, shall be your coast"* (Joshua 1:4).

Those are pretty clear instructions! God said, "I'll give you all the land from here to there, and from this point to that point." As long as they stayed within those boundaries and perimeters, they would be right in the middle of His divine plan and, therefore, could be assured of His divine assistance as they proceeded forward.

God did not promise to give them Egypt, Assyria, or other lands to the far north. He had made it very clear exactly which lands they were to possess. If they moved beyond those particular boundaries, then they could not be assured of success or God's assistance.

As long as they stayed where God had called them to be, they could be absolutely confident of supernatural help!

Biting Off More Than You Can Chew

One of the most embarrassing things to me is when a well-known minister or Christian businessman announces they are going to do something that sounds wonderful, and then they run out of money and cannot finish the job. It brings a reproach on the ministry and the Church.

In most cases when this happens, as good as their intentions may have been, they have wandered out of their primary calling into something God never called them to do, to meet a need He never called them to meet. Though there are exceptions, this is usually the case.

How many Christian schools have been started that God never initiated? How many well-meaning believers have started programs to feed the poor, when God only called them to teach His Word? How many people, truly called by God to have a radio or television ministry, have proceeded too hastily with their vision and then had to make desperate appeals for money because they had bitten off more than they could chew and couldn't pay the radio or television bills?

We've all seen it, we've all thought about it, and whether you are in business or ministry, you have probably done it! Just think of all the times you've started out with a budget for remodeling your house, moving to a new office, or just purchasing a few new articles of clothing. You know how easy it is to go beyond what you had planned to spend! In one way or another, we've all bitten off more than we could chew!

When it comes to having a mandate from God to reach masses of people, this is even easier to do. Seeing millions of people who desperately need to hear the gospel and the teaching of the Word of God, makes it extremely difficult — almost a heartbreaker — to say "no" to any opportunity to reach them for Christ.

There have been times when I had to say, "Someone else will have to do this, because I cannot be led by every need that I see, and I cannot afford to do any more at this moment." My greatest personal challenge right now is knowing when to say "All right, I'll accept another new region for television in the former USSR," and when to say, "We can't do anymore, enough is enough for now!"

When I see the great need and all the open doors before us, my natural inclination is to walk through every last one of them! There's just one problem. While the gospel is free for the lost, in some cases it takes a lot of money to preach it! Television time, production time, staff, stamps, churches, crusades, and printing literature all cost money and take a great investment of time and manpower.

Lack of vision has never been a problem to me! It is knowing how quickly or slowly to carry out the vision that has been my greatest challenge. In order to fulfill the dream God has put in my heart without making major errors that would create a financial crisis, I have to stay on my knees in prayer and constantly strive to be sensitive to the voice of the Holy Spirit.

I look at our financial books to see if we can handle another big assignment immediately. If I have a green light in my spirit to do a project, I'll do it by faith even if I don't know where the money is coming from. Most of the time, however, I have found that the Lord will leave it to me to make the decision based on what I have to work with in the natural — and that is probably coming as a shock to you!

Again, I go back to Proverbs 24:3-4, which tells us, *"Any enterprise is built by wise planning, becomes strong through common sense, and profits wonderfully by keeping abreast of the facts"* (TLB).

We must be people of both faith and common sense. Today this is a rare mixture indeed! If there is a huge open door that appears to be opened by the Lord, but there is no direct word from the Spirit in my heart to do it or not to do it, then I've got to do some serious thinking and praying before I make a decision.

Some decisions in life are based on a specific word from the Lord, but most of them are based on open doors and opportunities that are presented to us. By the use of plain old common sense, we determine which ones we need to walk through and which ones we cannot. Doesn't sound too spiritual, but that is often how God leads us.

I know it would be more exciting to be totally led by prophesies and visions during the night, but up to the moment of this writing, I don't know anyone in the world who is totally led in that way. Even the most well-known prophetic people in the Body of Christ do not base all their decisions on supernatural revelation.

Look at people who have succeeded! They are full of faith, courage, guts, brains, and common sense. They move ahead by faith, but when they have pushed their faith to the limit, and they know they are pushing too far and too fast, they stop, pray, and re-group. Later, when they are more confident, they begin moving ahead again.

What if the vision is very general, like our current word from God to teach His Word on television in the former USSR. That is a very large vision! It sounds like, "Go after all of it!" Hundreds of thousands of dollars are needed to do this, and when our financial resources are limited, then we have to take a common sense approach to fulfilling our vision. Carefully, step by step, we must allow the Holy Spirit to lead us.

You must not move ahead so fast that you don't have the cash flow to pay for your vision!

Again, this may not sound very spiritual, but the reality of serving God is this: Moving too fast without the resources to pay for your vision spells D-I-S-A-S-T-E-R ! ! !

Keep in mind that when the children of Israel passed over the Jordan River into the Promised Land, they didn't attempt to take the whole land all at once. They took it one piece at a time. Most likely, that is how you will fulfill your vision too — step by step. Just speaking honestly, most of us are probably not mature enough to handle it any quicker than that anyway!

Taking One Step at a Time

God had told Joshua, "*. . . go over this Jordan, thou, and all this people, unto the land which I do give to them, even to the children of Israel*" (Joshua 1:2).

If the children of Israel were like typical people today, they probably did a dance when they heard this prophetic word about crossing into the Land of Promise! I can almost hear them exclaiming, "It's here! Our day has come! He's giving us the land ! ! ! He's giving us the land ! ! !"

That is when God continued to tell them, "*Every place that the sole of your foot shall tread upon, that have I given unto you*" (Joshua 1:3).

God was going to give them their inheritance one step at a time. What wisdom on the part of God! Though it belonged to the Israelites by virtue of His promise, had they actually possessed the whole land immediately, it would have created all kinds of catastrophes. The land was so new to them, they needed time to understand it and know it.

God designed it so that they took each new territory as they walked across it and conquered it. Therefore, by the time they had possessed it, they had touched it, smelled it, examined it, searched it out, fought on it, and come to know it well. Putting their feet on that ground prepared them for managing it after it was theirs.

Had God dropped the whole thing into their laps, with no involvement of their part, they wouldn't have known what to do with it! They would have been totally over- whelmed by all the problems of every section of land all at the same time. What a mess!

It is the wisdom of God that success does not just fall out of the sky and land at our front door one morning. Step by step, we take the territory He has promised us. As we take each additional step, we become more acquainted with where God is calling us, and we become experienced. We begin to anticipate just what to expect when we take steps in the future.

We begin to see that each step we take is preparation for the next steps God will lead us to take tomorrow, the day after, and the day after that. Additionally, by taking our new territory one step at a time, we are able to deal with the challenges separately, individually, rather than taking on all the foes of hell and life at the same time!

If you stumble and fall the first couple of steps, that doesn't mean you have failed. You have just stumbled and fallen, like any child does when they first attempt to walk. Stumbling and falling in the beginning is a necessary phase of learning to walk.

You don't cry and weep when a baby falls after he takes his first steps! You just stand them back up and say, "Let's try it again!" Few babies hop to their feet one day and start walking. They crawl, then they pull themselves up to their feet by hanging onto a piece of furniture, and finally, with a somewhat terrified look in their eyes, they lift their foot to step forward for the first time!

After a few bruises and hard falls, eventually the day comes when the baby takes three or four steps in a row without falling. Even after they hit the floor after those steps, the exhilaration can still be seen on the baby's face at what they have done! To them, it's like climbing the world's tallest mountain.

For that baby to become a healthy child and adult, their development had to begin with those tiny steps. If the baby never attempted to crawl or walk, it is the doctor's signal that there is something wrong. Likewise, your first steps may seem huge and historic, but actually, the only thing really historic about them is that you took your first step of faith. They are historic because without them you wouldn't have been able to take all the other steps God has designed for your life.

If you have never taken a step of faith since you've been saved, it is a signal that something is very wrong with you spiritually. The Bible plainly teaches that the just shall live by faith (Habakkuk 2:4, Romans 1:17, Galatians 3:11, Hebrews 10:38). Because the Holy Spirit brings this to our attention again and again, I believe it has great significance!

You'll never know the thrill of living for God until you have stepped beyond your own abilities into the realm of faith. As one man said, "The just shall live by faith, and if he doesn't, then he doesn't ever really learn to live!"

When God said, *"Every place that the sole of your foot shall tread upon, that have I given unto you,"* He meant, "It's yours! Now come and get it! The minute you lay your feet on it, you can have it!"

Isn't it amazing how God requires us to grow and change as we move into each new assignment for our lives! He could have made it easy by just thrusting us forward quickly, or dropping new blessings into our lives with no involvement on our part. That, however, would defeat part of His purpose.

124

He doesn't just want to bless us, He wants to change us in the process of blessing us!

If those things we desire came to us too easily, no faith would be required, no crucifixion of our flesh would be demanded, and we would never personally grow or become conformed to the image of Jesus Christ.

God's plan for your life will not be finished until the conformity to His Son is complete. Romans 8:29 makes it very clear, *"For whom he did foreknow, he also did predestinate to be conformed to the image of his Son."*

With each new step of faith, God will reveal the flaws in your character that need to be put away. The Holy Spirit makes you aware of them, and then you must see that they are eliminated, or the phase of God's plan for your life you are in will not be fulfilled. By the time you are beyond that step, a new level of maturity will have been gained, which will enable you to take the next step more easily.

After time and experience, you will have enough life in God under your belt to make you wise enough and mature enough to accept the next really big challenge God will bring your way!

Be Specific and Realistic About Your Vision

God gave a very specific vision of the Promised Land to the children of Israel. He said, *"From the wilderness and this Lebanon even unto the great river, the river Euphrates, all the land of the Hittites, and unto the great sea toward the going down of the sun, shall be your coast"* (Joshua 1:4).

God knows we need clear directions in order to keep us on track. He didn't say, "Take any piece of land you want. Your inheritance is up to your own choosing!" Instead, His command was very pointed and clear, and nearly impossible to misinterpret. It was almost as though He told them, "From point A to point B is your ground, and no more!"

God gave the people direction and enabled them to set their sight on something concrete. They had a goal to shoot for as they crossed over into that land. He knew that human beings need direction and purpose. When people have nothing to look forward to, nothing to work toward, they tend to wander or they begin to set their own agendas.

It is the nature of human beings to want discipline, boundaries, borders, and goals for their lives. Without them, they become drunkards or create confusion by trying to set a direction and find their purpose for themselves.

Children want boundaries and, when their parents do not set boundaries for them, in the end those children end up hating and disrespecting their parents. First Samuel 3:13 teaches us that Eli destroyed his sons because he didn't love them enough to set boundaries for their lives and discipline them. Proverbs 13:24 clearly warns us to be sure to set clear boundaries for our children and discipline them, that it is the equivalent of hating them and assuring them of a future filled with destruction if we don't.

When leaders do not give clear goals and direction to their organizations, they are opening the door for failure, discouragement, depression, poverty, and faithlessness in their people. They also may be leaving the door open for someone in the organization to step forward and say, "If no one else will lead you and give you direction, then look to me! I will!"

Most organizational and church splits could have been avoided had the leadership been more specific and focused on the future. People need something to look toward! If you don't provide it, they will find something or someone else to lead them or something else to focus on. History should teach us this!

Proverbs 29:18 says, *"Where there is no vision, the people perish: but he that keepeth the law, happy is he."*

People need purpose and a plan for their lives. If they do not have it, they will never become all they were intended to be. If you are a father or mother, take time to give your children something to shoot for! Impart dreams of greatness to them! Help them to see themselves as being godly leaders further on in their lives.

If you own a business, set goals for your staff and sales people. Don't expect them to be the visionaries of your company. You are their leader! They need your vision, your faith, and your ideas about the future. Help them to see where your company is headed and what the dividends will be for those who are faithful.

If you are a pastor, you need to ask God what His plan is for your congregation and declare that vision to them. The nation is speckled with thousands of little churches that will never do anything significant because they have no direction. Don't let that be your church!

God called you and your people to do more than just come to a building to see one another, sing a few songs, and hear a nice message once a week. You can change the history of your city and the surrounding area if you will get God's vision for your church and begin carrying it out with everything you've got!

Occasionally, I hear young preachers say, "We're going to take the whole world for Jesus!" Be realistic! You are not going to take the whole world for Jesus, and even if you did, you wouldn't know what to do with it when you finished taking it! You might take a part of the world for Jesus, but you personally, your ministry, or your church, are never going to take the whole world for Jesus. It is ridiculous to even make such a statement!

The Apostle Peter was specifically called to the Jewish world, and the Apostle Paul was specifically called to the Gentile world. When these men tried to move beyond those boundaries and cross over into each other's territory, they nearly always encountered problems. They had gone beyond the place where God had called them to be and stepped out of His provision and protection.

Rather than focus on a vision that is so broad, be more specific about your vision. What part of the world does God want you to reach? By what means are you supposed to reach it? God didn't tell Joshua, "Here is the world, young man! It's all yours!" Instead, He gave very clear boundaries and limitations to Joshua as he and the Israelites moved into the Promised Land.

If you live in a city of several million people, even half a million people, I seriously doubt God is going to give you the whole city, but He will give you a portion of the city! Which part of the city does God wish to give you? The north side? The south side? The east side? The west side? Maybe He wants to give you the central region, or the youth center, the nursing home, the senior citizens, the homeless, the high school students, or the executive community.

Whatever God has given you, go get it!

Praying to Get the Divine Strategy

Prayer is essential to making your vision happen. Not only is it the only way you are going to know the specific boundaries and perimeters of your vision, but it is the only way you can find out how, when, where, and with whom you are to proceed.

You are not going to open your Bible one day and read, "Joe Smith shall take the City of Gnaw Bone, Indiana, for God. He will establish a church on Main Street the first year, over the following three years he will add a children's school housed in the warehouse across the street from the church and hire Brother Jones to run it, and then in June of 1994 he will start a Bible school. . . ."

To get that kind of specific direction, you are going to have to spend some time with the Holy Spirit, and He usually only gives you the plan one step at a time! What is the next practical step God wants you and your church to take to bring Jesus Christ to the people of your city? How do you move forward? How do you put your foot on that ground and claim it for your own?

One thing is certain, it will never happen by sitting in the four walls of your church building and praying for the city to become yours. I've seen hundreds of churches who have made the mistake of believing revival would come to them. On the contrary, if you want to reach your city for Jesus Christ, then in addition to praying, you've got to get out of your church building and get them!

One of the reasons we pray about revival in our churches is not just for God to pour out His Spirit, but also to get His divine strategy and plan to achieve it!

Charismatic churches tend to do more praying than acting. They pray with the greatest of intensity, which is wonderful and a great example for all of us to follow. *Prayer is the foundation for revival!* Every major revival in history has been preceded by a strong season of prayer in the Church. But even with all of their intense praying, most charismatic churches remain small through the years.

While they pray with the greatest of intensity, they many times lack a strategy to see that revival come about. There are exceptions, of course, and those churches who are exceptions, who do have a strategy, who have a step-by-step plan on how to affect their city and the whole nation, are usually the fastest growing churches in the country. Everyone takes note of them and wonders how they have done it!

Most Baptist churches, on the other hand, are more aggressive in evangelism than most charismatic churches, and they have a reputation for growing steadily through the years. I have heard charismatic pastors all over the nation talk about how remarkable it is that Baptist churches are so constant in their growth patterns.

There is a reason for the consistency of their growth patterns. They work as hard as they can to reach their cities for Jesus Christ! They have visitation nights, work days, schedules for when they call everyone on their membership roll to remind them of the vision of reaching the lost. The vision is always set before the congregation.

Yet being a former Southern Baptist and having served in a pastoral capacity in one large Southern Baptist church, I am well aware that their prayer emphasis is not as bold as their charismatic brothers'. Without the understanding of prayer and hearing from the Holy Spirit about a matter, it is very easy to do what man has deemed effective, according to the traditions of men, when it is not God's way for that time and place.

You've got to have the spiritual side and the practical side to achieve victory in any area of life.

Just praying in general terms is not enough — you've got to ask the Holy Spirit for a specific, detailed strategy and then begin to do what He tells you to do. If all you do is work a plan that seems right or that your denomination has always used, then you are not operating from a spiritual foundation and you have no support for what you are trying to achieve.

You've got to build a foundation to sustain your vision, and prayer will build that foundation. Start with a dream, a word from the Lord, and then pray with all of your might. Once you know what you are supposed to do and how you are supposed to do it, put all your mind, heart, strength, and energy into the assignment.

Pray like the success of the whole project depends completely on God, but work like the success of the whole project depends completely on you!

This powerful combination of prayer and hard work always produces marvelous fruit in the kingdom of God. If you are in the business world and you desire to move further ahead in your company or profession, how are you going to do it? Sitting at your desk and simply thinking about your future will not accomplish anything.

You've got to start out by praying and dreaming, asking the Holy Spirit to impart a plan, an idea, an objective, a strategy to get from where you are to where you want to be. That new assignment at your company will not come to you by itself. You've got to take one step at a time, steadily moving toward your goal, until, finally, your goal is realized and that place of promotion is yours at last!

Allowing God to Expand Your Boundaries and Diminish Your Limitations

I seriously doubt that a janitor of a company, who has this wild, outrageous dream of becoming the president of that company one day, will be promoted directly from the janitor's department to the president's office. His vision is big and exciting, and that's great, but how is he going to get from the cleaning closet to the executive lounge?

If you are a student who only makes average grades, and you want to do better, how are you going to achieve that? If you are a father or mother, and you want to be a better parent, how are you going to improve your skills in parenting?

If you feel like you are failing as a wife or husband and you want save your marriage, you truly want to be the best spouse you can possibly be, then you have a huge challenge in front of you. It is rare that we achieve these goals overnight. How are you going to do it? What are you going to do? How are you going to get from point A to point B?

Be more specific in the way that you pray, and ask God, "How do I proceed to move toward the goal You have put in my heart?" In addition to giving you a general, broad, huge vision, now He will begin to give you smaller visions, ideas, steps to take that will slowly and steadily take you toward your goal.

God told Joshua and the children of Israel that the Land of Promise would be theirs as they took it step by step. That is exactly how God will give you your future too, step by step. The beauty of this method is that with each step, you will change and grow. Your vision will get a little bigger and you will have a little more confidence about the power of the Holy Spirit working in your life to accomplish what you used to think was impossible.

While each step seems tiny at the moment, if you turn around and look at where you are right now, compared to where you used to be about five steps back, you probably won't even recognize your old self! It's amazing how all those tiny steps bring forth a radical transformation!

If your thinking is small right now, it won't take too much of a vision to really begin stretching you! For instance, if you live in a small town and you've never been out of your state, taking a trip to New York City might sound like the greatest adventure imaginable! You might even feel like you've conquered the world (at least the Big Apple!) because you've done something so brave and daring.

That one experience just changed your perspective of the world. Now you have seen life beyond your home town. You've just seen a part of life you've never seen before. When you are finished seeing other parts of the United States, then parts of Europe, and perhaps even other parts of the world, your perspective will be radically changed again and again.

When you return to your home town, you will realize how small your world had been in that period of your life. How unfortunate to see only our little circle, our little home town, and miss the whole of what God has for our lives. But that is what people tend to do!

The vision God places in your heart will always amount to something bigger than you, something that you cannot do without the help of the Holy Spirit. Prayerfully and diligently, you can only begin with small steps, one at a time, which are all orchestrated of the Lord.

If you walk in those steps, you will grow and mature and change and expand, and then look back, in absolute awe of the way the Holy Spirit has brought you from a tiny little step of faith to the giant leaps you are taking today!

Success, joy, and fulfillment begin with knowing God's specific plan for your life, then pursuing that plan prayerfully, working in the boundaries and perimeters He has set for you, asking the Holy Spirit for the divine strategy to carry it out, taking one step of faith at a time, and growing and expanding all through the process.

Then, as you move ahead in obedience and faith, you'll find the greatest and most delightful surprise of all! God's Spirit is working alongside of you with supernatural wisdom and power beyond your wildest dreams!

Chapter Seven
Be Strong and Courageous!

Where did Joshua get his strength and courage? Before he marched toward the Jordan River, God spoke to him, *"There shall not any man be able to stand before thee all the days of thy life: as I was with Moses, so I will be with thee: I will not fail thee, nor forsake thee"* (Joshua 1:5).

That's an incredible promise!

"There shall not any man be able to stand before thee all the days of thy life!" When we know we are in the middle of God's will for our lives and doing what He has specifically asked us to do, regardless of the opposition, the situations, or the problems, no human being or earthly circumstance is big enough to stop what we've been called to do.

As He was with Moses! Really? He will be with me in the same way He was with Moses? That's exactly what God told Joshua. If we are reading this promise right (and we are!) He will part the Red Sea, the Jordan River, or any other obstacle in order to help us get the job done! With God on our side, we can be sure of victory.

God continued to promise, *"I will not fail thee, or forsake thee."* With knowledge that all the power of heaven is at your side, why not throw off all those forces that hinder you and start taking the first necessary steps toward fulfilling God's plan for your life!

What about opposition? Everyone has it! Even if you stayed home, watched television, and did nothing all day, you would never eliminate or escape opposition in your life. This is what will happen if you do: You will grow fat, lazy, and very unattractive to your spouse, and have serious marriage problems. You will never do anything exciting, and will thus become critical of those who do. Your children will watch your behavior, duplicate you, and become totally unproductive with no incentive for their lives. Then, when you wish they would grow up and move out of the house, they won't!

Doing nothing doesn't eliminate opposition, it just creates a different kind of opposition!

You might as well choose the kind of opposition you want to face in life. Do you want problems that result from doing nothing, or do you want challenges that result from tackling what others call impossible! I've already made my choice. The amazing and gratifying thing is, I'm seeing my children begin to dream! They are already in the formative stages of making their choices and seeing God's plan for their lives, too!

You can take God's words to Joshua and make them your own today: *"No man will be able to stand before me all the days of my life. As God was with Moses, so He will be with me. He will not fail me, nor forsake me!"*

Leadership Crisis in the Church Today

When Joshua became the new leader of Israel, the nation was in a leadership crisis. For thirty days Moses had been dead and the people were wondering, "Who will lead us? Who will show us where to go? Who will speak to God on our behalf?"

In the midst of this instability, the word of the Lord came to Joshua, calling him into the position of leadership for which he had been training many years. The Lord spoke to him, *"Be strong and of a good courage: for unto this people shalt thou divide for an inheritance the land, which I sware unto their fathers to give them"* (Joshua 1:6).

Notice particularly God's opening command to Joshua: *"Be strong and of a good courage. . ."* If anything is needed today, it is leaders who are willing to take a stand and who are willing to do what is right, regardless of whether or not it is politically correct. Leaders who are strong and courageous are very scarce, both in the world and in the Church.

We live in a time when no one wants to offend anyone else, no one wants to make critical decisions or to take a stand that might jeopardize their own future job security. This is precisely what is wrong with politics in western nations like the United States of America. For the most part, no one is willing to lead, because no one wants to offend.

Everybody tries to walk on glass when they first become the leader, because they want to be liked and they don't want to offend anybody. They want to be the friend of the people. There is no such thing if you are a leader! Not everybody is going to like you or appreciate you or agree with you all the time. If you try to please everyone, you will please no one, and you certainly won't please God.

What if you make a decision that offends someone? What if you make a statement that is not politically correct? What if you make a special interest group angry and, in the next election, they oppose your reelection? What if? What if? What if ! ! !

So-called leaders in politics are so controlled by the fear of man that their leadership is paralyzed from the moment it begins. Politicians become tossed to and fro by special interest groups who give them money to finance their reelection campaigns. They forget they were sent to the Congress to represent the people.

Because no one wants to offend anyone else, no one wants to appear to be a bigot or offend a sexual minority group that has amazing political clout, elected officials are paralyzed in their ability to lead. They owe so many favors to so many people, even before they are elected the special interest groups control them.

These are not leaders. These are politicians.

The common people can normally smell them out and would love to get rid of them, but money from special groups keeps them in place year after year. In the end, it creates a sour taste in the mouths of voters, who wonder, "Why do we even vote anyway? Those we elect seem to only represent the fringe of society. Is our vote really worth anything?"

We are in a great leadership crisis today — especially in the United States of America — and a leadership crisis in the nation comes from a leadership crisis in the family and the fabric of social relationships in the community.

Husbands do not want to lead for fear of offending and losing a spouse. Fathers and mothers are afraid to discipline their children for fear of being accused of child abuse. Employers are afraid to hire the person who is the most qualified for the job because they will be labeled a racist.

Teachers in school do not want to take authority in the classroom because someone might claim that their rights are being violated. Rather than teach that sex before marriage is a sin and offend some nonreligious organization, condoms are given to kids in high school. Children now have the right to divorce their parents should they not like the way things are going at home.

We are in a great leadership crisis today in our nation! The same pattern of decline and disintegration that existed in classical Greece and in the Roman Empire right before their fall is now in motion here in the "home of the free and the brave."

In the same way there is a leadership crisis in political circles today, there is a terrible, gaping hole of leadership in the Church. Just like the world, it seems believers are afraid to take a stand for fear of hurting someone else's feelings.

As a result, whole congregations and even leaders sit by and tolerate things that should never be tolerated!

Pastors are afraid of their board of advisors, afraid of what would happen if they told the worship leader to change the way he or she is leading worship, afraid to offend church members for fear that they will leave the church and quit giving to the budget, and so on. Of course, this is not true of every pastor, but far too many nonetheless.

Some pastors are afraid to take offerings, so they put a little box in the back of the church and hope and pray someone will put some money in there on their way out. But there never was a box in the temple, because offerings were always part of worshipping the Lord, and we need not ever apologize for asking the people for money. God asked for every bit of gold the children of Israel had when it was time to build the tabernacle!

Leaders in the Body of Christ need to walk in that kind of boldness, but that kind of boldness hinges on one central truth: *Who you fear will determine the decisions you make!*

If you fear the opinion of man, then the fear of man will dictate your decisions. If, on the other hand, you fear a holy God Whom you know you will stand before one day, that fear of God will control and dictate your decisions.

I was once a pastor in the United States, and I am now pastoring a church in Riga, Latvia. Thus, I understand the subtle fears that can nearly overtake you before you even realize you're under attack!

Moreover, as a traveling Bible teacher who gained some recognition, I know what it's like to teach something that may not prove popular with your fellow ministers. I know the paranoia that stems from the fear of man, always wondering if you'll be rejected for taking a stand that no one else seems to want to take, or for teaching something that is not in agreement with what everyone else is running toward at the time.

The fear of man was blatantly exposed in my life when the Lord instructed me to write **Merchandising the Anointing**. As a matter of fact, though many people were helped and blessed by that book, I believe the primary purpose of that book was for me! It exposed something in me that I didn't know was in me: the fear of man!

As that book rolled off the press, my telephone began to ring from all across the nation. Leaders were saying, "Please don't print that book. Let's just forget all the crazy doctrines that are being taught right now and let's walk in love with one another."

The reason I wrote the book was *because* I was walking in love! *I love the Church!* The Church was more important to God than how I stood in the current popular opinion poll — and I am convinced that He was clearly leading me to take a stand that needed to be taken. But writing that book revealed a need to submit my will and my emotions to the power of God, and to break the spirit of fear that was secretly trying to operate in my life.

Magnify that a million times in the life of a pastor who has to hear the constant murmurings, complainings, and opinions of the people. As wonderful as the sheep of God are, there are times when they can really act like goats, kicking and butting every direction!

The amazing thing is, every person with an opinion is certain that their opinion is the right one, or that they have really heard from the Lord! Here is the problem: when that church has four hundred people who vary in their opinions and they are all certain their opinion is right and is directed by the Lord, it doesn't matter what decision the pastor makes, he is going to offend someone! There is no way to get around trouble for that man of God!

He might as well go ahead and do what God has instructed him to do, because he's never going to be able to please all those people! Love them and listen to them if you wish, but in the end, go ahead and lead them. That's what they want you to do anyway.

When a leader never takes a stand or gives direction, it is difficult and frustrating for the people to follow them. But the truth is, even if they don't agree with your direction, if you lead them with guts, boldness, and courage, they will support you anyway, because they respect your willingness to take a stand!

A Common Trait of All Great World Leaders

I now live in the former Soviet Union and, as I have traveled all across this land and have spoken to Russians, Ukrainians, Baltic peoples, and other nationalities about their deadly and bloody past national history, I am totally amazed that men like Stalin were so respected and followed wholeheartedly during their ruthless reign. Why?

Why would a whole nation follow a man so devilish in his deeds? Why would a people follow someone who was murdering their families, neighbors, and countrymen? Why did the Soviet Union mourn so deeply when this mass murderer died in 1953? Why?

The answer to this question is no great secret. He was a strong leader.

They followed him for the identical reason Nazi Germany followed a madman named Hitler.

They followed him for the same reason the nation of France followed Napoleon in his insane dream to conquer Europe.

They followed him for the same reason all the peoples of the Roman Empire worshipped their most treacherous emperors.

They followed him for one of the same reasons that the children of Israel followed Moses.

They followed him for the same reason that the people of the United States reelected Franklin D. Roosevelt to four terms as President of the United States.

They followed them for the same reason England looked to Winston Churchill through World War II.

Though these leaders are very different from one another and hold different philosophies and ideologies, they all had one thing in common: *they led.*

They may not have always led the people in the right direction, and some of them even led wickedly, but they led with strength and confidence — and that's what people always have and always will look for and respond to with total allegiance.

Even if their political opinions were wrong and badly off-track, no one ever questioned where they stood on an issue, no one ever wondered if they were willing to take a stand, and no one ever wondered if they were afraid of the opinions of man. *They led!*

It is estimated that Stalin's governmental policies ended up killing between forty and sixty million people during his reign of terror in the Soviet Union. Yet, on the day he died, more than fifteen hundred people were crushed to death trying to get to the Kremlin to see their beloved Comrade Stalin lying in state. He was adored. Why?

Even with all of his wicked behavior, he led the people from a financially wrecked revolutionary period to a period of stability and control. When Hitler challenged the Soviet Union, Stalin met the challenge with the same strength and courage, further increasing his position of absolute power in the minds of Soviet citizens. Because he was so strong, he was a focal point of security, strength, and guidance.

The same could be said of Hitler. As wicked as he was in his doctrines, his leadership style was so strong that he provided the leadership no one else was willing to give at the moment. At a moment in German history when the economy was literally collapsing and inflation was out of control, with no end in sight to the problems, this man rose to a place of power by giving strong leadership to a people who were desperate for leadership. *He led.*

Where there is a vacuum of leadership, instability is the result. When that instability becomes rampant, so rampant that no one wants to take a stand on any issue and anarchy begins to spread throughout the nation, eventually people become weary of it all and want to return to a state where someone gives them purpose and direction. This is the perfect environment for terrible dictators to emerge.

It is also the golden moment for you to hear God and step forward to answer the call! The Body of Christ is crying out for leadership right now!

Let me ask you this question: have you ever visited a huge church, where you have to search and search for a parking place before the service begins because there are so many members? Then, when the service finally begins, you sadly realize it is one of the most boring church services you have ever attended in your whole life!

I've been to a few services like that. It's always the most amazing thing to me. I watch them, hundreds and even thousands of people, hurriedly rushing to attend one of the most boring meetings you would ever experience!

What's even more amazing is to see how committed the people are to faithfully attend each service, never missing, and how they faithfully give of their tithes and offerings. Yet the church services are basically dead and uneventful.

The pastor talks in nearly a monotone, with no special preaching or teaching ability. The members look joyless as they hold their hymnbooks, and the choir stands on the platform like statues. By the time the invitation is finished, everyone in the whole place is loaded with so much condo-bondo (condemnation and bondage) that they hardly crack a smile when they tell everyone farewell until next Sunday.

On a few occasions, I've been invited to preach in churches like this. Often, before I preach, I have the chance to sit and watch in an earlier service so I can experience the church and know exactly what kind of congregation I will be ministering to that day. If it's a church like this, I nearly always think to myself, why do all these people come here Sunday after Sunday? What motivates them to keep giving their tithes and offerings when they can't even smile at church? What is it about this church that attracts so many people to come here?

In most of the cases the answer is the same. The pastor is a strong leader. He may not be the most exciting preacher you've ever heard in your life, but he is steady, strong, bold, courageous, and unwavering in his leadership style.

You might not agree with his dogmatic, unyielding, almost merciless doctrine, but you definitely know where he stands on issues. There are no grey areas, no questionable things about his lifestyle or behavior. He is just exactly what you see: *strong, steady, unwavering.*

People keep coming because that pastor has a strong personality that emanates strength to the congregation. Even if his preaching does put you to sleep, one thing is not debatable: the pastor is in charge, is imparting his vision to the church, and is demanding commitment of his members.

In fact, his leadership is so strong, people are able to follow it! No one doubts where this pastor stands or where he intends to lead his church in the future.

Weak Leaders Versus Strong Leaders

God told Joshua, *"Be strong . . ."*

People need to see strength in a leader. This is the main thing people are looking for in leadership. They are not really looking for someone who is perfect and never makes a mistake, but someone who can give them direction. They want strength in a leader.

This is the reason weak leaders eventually lose their businesses and congregations. This is the reason nations despise weak politicians. If they cannot make decisions and then stick with them, if they are prone to waver back and forth, and if they are so easily influenced by special interest groups that they are always changing their views and beliefs to accommodate others, they will lose the respect of their followers, whether a congregation, a staff, or a nation.

Be strong! Pray and discover God's plan for your life, your family, your church, your business, your state, your nation, and then make up your mind to do what God has put in your heart. Make that announcement with faith, and then stay in faith! Establish your heart on what God has said and never waver in front of the people.

Even if you feel a little shaky on the inside about the decision you have made, keep that to yourself. You don't need to tell everything you think and feel to the people you are leading. If they see fear and instability in you, it will undermine your ability to lead. Don't tell them so much about what you are thinking and feeling that they cease to see you as a leader and begin to simply see you as a fellow struggler, also uncertain about what direction to take.

Let them think you are strong, even if you are feeling weak. If you have a need to tell someone that you are going through a struggle, then tell it to a dear, long-standing friend, who has seen you struggle and make it before. They will know how to encourage you.

Tell it to your parents, tell it to your spouse, tell it to a faithful friend, tell it to your pastor, but don't spill your guts to the whole congregation or to all the people who work for you in your business or ministry. If you do that, you will scare the life out of them!

Put that smile back on your face and fake it! Remember, your emotions are temporary, and it probably won't take too long until your confidence and joy return. How pitiful to spill your guts about your fears and anxieties and then, when your fears dissipate and your faith returns, you have a whole church, business, family, or ministry who are affected — maybe deeply affected — by the temporary feelings of fear and anxiety you dumped on them.

There is a time for you to keep your mouth shut and to put on a happy face, even if you don't feel too happy.

You are a leader! You don't have the privilege of showing the same kind of weakness other people show. You can bare your heart to your closest friends and family if you must, but don't show your doubts and fears to the people whom you are leading. Most of them will not be able to handle it!

God continues to clarify this point to Joshua by saying, "*. . . for unto this people shalt thou divide for an inheritance the land, which I sware unto their fathers to give them.*"

Notice that He says, "*. . . for unto this people . . .*" Why is this important? Because it reminds us that our leadership is connected to people!

Joshua's new calling in life connected him to people! Simply by virtue of the word "leader," leaders are people who lead *people*. A pastor without a congregation ceases to be a pastor. A husband without a wife ceases to be a husband. A father or mother without children ceases to be a father or mother. A president without a nation ceases to be a president.

Leadership is not derived from an official title, but from a relationship to people.

God wanted Joshua to know that his leadership was connected to people, so He said, "*Be strong and courageous, for unto this people . . .*" If Joshua failed to give them the strength and courage they needed to follow him over the Jordan River and into the Promised Land, then he failed to be the leader God wanted him to be.

When God calls you to accept a new assignment in life, it is going to require you to move into a new realm of faith, courage, and boldness. You probably won't feel prepared for it, but God has counted you faithful enough to handle it, or the door would not have opened to you. You can do it!

A daily time of prayer and study in the Word of God, constantly keeping yourself in remembrance of God's revealed plan for your life, your family, ministry, or your business, and projecting the strength and confidence people need to see in you will bring great reward. You can lead your people through all the challenges, difficulties, and problems — right into the middle of the Promised Land!

Turn Not to the Right or the Left

In Joshua 1:7, God exhorts Joshua, *"Only be thou strong and very courageous, that thou mayest observe to do according to all the law, which Moses my servant commanded thee: turn not from it to the right hand or to the left, that thou mayest prosper whithersoever thou goest."*

God desires careful obedience!

He doesn't want you going this way or that way when He tells you to do something and gives you very specific instructions. He wants you to do it exactly the way He instructed you to do it. When He told Moses how to build the tabernacle, He gave the most intricate construction plan. There is so much sloppy obedience in the Church today, I wonder if we could build that tabernacle!

We need unwavering commitment that we will not stray from the word God speaks to us, not turning to the right or the left, but doing exactly as He directs us.

You will have plenty of opportunities to fudge on a word from God! And do you know what? You may find another route that looks great and may even be very good, but if it is not exactly what God said, don't you dare turn to it! Be wary of people who say, "Do you really think that's what the Lord meant? You know you could interpret that two ways. I know what you think the Lord said, but let's consider this. We would not be sensible if we refused to consider other options."

147

I have heard these words so many times! You are foolish if you consider other options or any other alternative to what God has spoken to you. Who in the world do we think we are to look for a better way than what God has commanded?

Notice what the Scripture goes on to say, "... *that thou mayest prosper whithersoever thou goest.*" When you do what God has asked you to do and you honor Him by doing it His way, seeking His perfect will in every aspect of it, you will prosper.

When I obeyed God and sent 25,000 teaching tapes all over the world to missionaries, and I did it His way, great prosperity came to our ministry like never before. Our meetings increased, our funds increased, the strength of our relationships with pastors and churches increased, and our personal finances increased.

I don't even want to think about what we would have forfeited had we not obeyed the Lord in this, but I could have! I could have only sent out 10,000 or 15,000. I could have sent them to a few missionaries and distributed the rest in the United States. But, thank God, we didn't! We knew when God spoke that there was prosperity in His Word to us, that if we obeyed Him and honored Him, great prosperity would manifest.

An Important Command

This was to be the first of three times God would speak these same words to Joshua, "*Be strong and of a good courage.*" In verse 6, God said, "*Be strong and of a good courage.*" In verse 7, He said, "*Be strong and very courageous.*" Then, in verse 9, He said, "*Have I not commanded thee? Be strong, and of a good courage.*"

Joshua must have been thinking, "Yes, yes, yes! I hear You and I get the message! You want me to be strong and courageous!" But why did God continue repeating these words to him? *Because these are the most important elements of leadership.* Notice that He didn't tell Joshua three times that he should pray or meditate or keep the vision in front of him. That doesn't mean these things are not important, but they are not the *most important* element in leadership.

God always repeats something for the sake of driving a point home. What is the first thing God requires of you? Strength. Leaders must be strong. Why? Because ministry is hard, whether God has called you to drive a school bus, be a college professor, run a company, or be a pastor. The enemy does not want the kingdom of God to advance, he is against you, and he will incite other people to be against you — sometimes even those who are dear to you.

There's a price to pay to serve God, no matter who you are, or how high on the ladder you go. Therefore, you must be strong.

Remember how a leader is in a relationship with the people he leads? A true leader is someone who is always using his strength to encourage and build up others. He is always propping people up. There is something in him so strong that people draw courage from him.

Being strong and courageous doesn't mean you promote yourself so everybody will know how anointed you are. It means you use your strength to encourage and lead the people. That's why the very next statement after *"Be strong and of a good courage"* says, *"for unto this people."* Your strength and courage are for the people! Strength and courage manifest encouragement!

Without consistently showing strength and courage and imparting encouragement to those who follow you, you can pray, meditate and study the Word of God, and ponder your vision night and day, but you will fail as a leader.

After God had finished talking with Joshua, Joshua turned to the officers of the people and gave them the Lord's instructions. As he stepped into his role as their leader, all the commanders came before Joshua and said, *"All that thou commandest us we will do, and whithersoever thou sendest us, we will go.*

"According as we hearkened unto Moses in all things, so will we hearken unto thee: only the Lord thy God be with thee, as he was with Moses.

"Whosoever he be that doth rebel against thy commandment, and will not hearken unto thy words in all that thou commandest him, he shall be put to death" (Joshua 1:16-18).

Most pastors and business leaders, husbands, wives, parents, and company directors would give anything for that kind of dedication!

"Yes Pastor, we will do anything you ask us to do. We will go anywhere you tell us to go. We will hearken unto every word you speak to us. In fact, we are so committed to following you that, if anyone in this church disobeys you and refuses to follow your commands, we'll kill them!"

Whew! That is loyalty and faithfulness of the highest, most sought-after magnitude! Can you imagine what Joshua must have been thinking at the moment? "Look at me! I'm quite a leader! They love me so much, they would kill if I asked them to! My leadership ability is so strong, they will go where I say to go and they will do what I tell them to do."

Then, right in the midst of Joshua's exultation about how well things were going so far, his commanders end by saying, *"ONLY BE STRONG AND OF A GOOD COURAGE."*

Now wait a minute! God already said that in verse 6, repeated it in verse 7, and spoke it again in an even stronger tone, as a commandment, in verse 9. Now, in verse 18, He says it again — through the mouths of the people whom Joshua is called to lead! Joshua must have thought, "Were they listening when God spoke to me?"

Even the people knew that God said, *"Be strong and of a good courage!"* They were willing to follow Joshua, obey him, even kill for him, but all they wanted from him was clear, precise, strong, and courageous leadership. In other words, "If you will really lead, then we will really follow."

As You Embark on Your Next Assignment

As you strike out to tackle your next new assignment in life, look at the first chapter of Joshua and consider every point God spoke to Joshua's heart.

The waters before you may look dangerously wild and torrid, the people you are called to lead may bring problems and challenges, and the Promised Land God has set before you may be filled with conflict as well as blessing. However, if you step forward with courage, you will enter into a new realm of miraculous living that you have never experienced!

Pick up your feet and take that first step into the unknown! That's where your faith will explode and the adventure will take off. You will never know the joy of truly serving God in a life of faith by sitting at home, watching television, avoiding new challenges in life, and ignoring the voice of the Holy Spirit deep in your heart.

Once the children of Israel hearkened unto the voice of Joshua and stepped into the Jordan River, the Bible says, *"And the priests that bare the ark of the covenant of the Lord stood firm on dry ground in the midst of Jordan, and all the Israelites passed over on dry ground, until all the people were passed clean over Jordan"* (Joshua 3:17).

I am certain everyone shouted for joy when the waters parted and they passed over on dry ground. But no one rejoiced more than Joshua, for this miracle was God's proof and sign that Joshua was His choice to lead the nation of Israel during the next phase of His plan.

This miracle accomplished something else. It gave the people another dose of faith and encouragement that they were right on track. And just as the parting of the Red Sea had encouraged them in the wilderness, remembering the parting of the Jordan River would sustain them when they reached the next crossroads of faith, the next point of no return.

If you have established your heart on God's personal promises to you, and dedicated your whole life to bringing forth the dream and vision He has placed in you, then you will reach the point of no return many times! Tackle each new assignment in God's plan for your life with faith, strength, courage, confidence, boldness, and common sense, and . . .

Welcome to a life of living in The Point of No Return!